All That Is Not Given Is Lost

Also by Greg Kuzma

Something at Last Visible (1969)
Sitting Around (1969)
Eleven Poems (1971)
The Bosporus (1971)
Harry's Things (1971)
Poems (1971)
Song for Someone Going Away and Other Poems (1971)
Good News (1973)
What Friends Are For (1973)
A Problem of High Water (1973)
The Buffalo Shoot (1974)
The Obedience School (1974)
A Day in the World (1976)
Nebraska (1977)
Garden Report (1977)
Adirondacks (1978)
Village Journal (1978)
For My Brother (1981)
Everyday Life (1983)
A Horse of a Different Color (1983)
Of China and Of Greece (1984)
A Turning (1988)
Wind Rain and Stars and the Grass Growing (1993)
Grandma (1995)
What Poetry is All About (1998)
Getting the Dead Out (2001)

All
That
Is
Not
Given
Is
Lost

Greg Kuzma

The Backwaters Press

Cover design by Bristol Creative, www.bristolcreative.com

Book design by The Backwaters Press

Author photo by Barbara Kuzma, ©2007

First printing May, 2007

The Backwaters Press
Greg Kosmicki, Rich Wyatt, Editors
3502 North 52nd Street
Omaha, Nebraska 68104-3506

gkosmicki@cox.net
www.thebackwaterspress.homestead.com

ISBN: 0-9785782-7-9

Thanks to these editors and publishers for permission to reprint here.

Crazyhorse: "How I Got My Name"

The Iowa Review: "The Spider on the Windowsill"

The Lincoln Review: "In the Library"

The Midwest Quarterly: "Arguments," "Reciting 'The Highwayman,' "
     "Photograph of My Mother Playing Pinochle," "Reading
     Student Poems," "Burning the Candle at Both Ends,"
     "Robbing Peter to Pay Paul," "And If I Had a Lever Long
     Enough I Would Move the Earth," "Bill," "Drinking Beer
     with Bill Trela," and "Getting the Dead Out"

Poetry East: "Warren"

Triquarterly: "The Arrangement"

"Grandma" was published as a chapbook by Best Cellar Press.

Contents

For my father, Harry Kuzma,
for Bill Kuzma,
and for Jeff
"brothers I loved you all"

Arguments

I write this while my father is
alive. "Hallelujah," I can hear him say.
"Thank God for small favors."
He is old now, but continually surprising.
That is good, is it not? to be amazed at
one's father, "rounding the Horn," on his
way to seventy and counting. A son
modifies a father. Once he stood before me,
blocking my way to the world. It was all
a bluff. Fighting every inch to get here,
when I got past him it was just the
world, and nothing he knew about. He
ran into his house and hid, like a
terrible troll, up out from under
the bridge, now that no one was afraid of him.
Our struggles were all with each other.
It was as if we wished to occupy the
same body, the same air. I recall our
fevered arguments. They would start civil
enough— "Well, how was school?" he would
ask. And could I make a plain reply?
No chance. I'd watch his eye and try
to say a word to make it jump.
Whatever it would take, I'd even lie,
just to shake him up. Oh the cruelties
we practice on each other. And, unthinking,
we do not wonder who will love us,
only how to piss somebody off.
And come back later to be forgiven,
like a pup for digging under the fence,
and running wild. To take one's

bowl of water and food, and curl
beside a father's chair. The veins
in his head would stand out, his face
would flush. We knew exactly
what it was was over much, and
always crossed the line, into
forbidden zones. That's the fun of
a thing though, to take a chance,
to risk the world, when nothing really
mattered after all. The next morning
he'd be back outside before I got up,
enmeshed in his chores, and Sunday
afternoon I'd be gone again, back to
school. He'd be the one to drive
me back. We'd go a long way,
unspeaking, maybe the radio on.
I don't recall we ever mentioned
anything we'd said, to indicate
perhaps we'd done some further
thinking. That was the world
then. And all the time his life
was falling down. I know that now.
A father myself, I've driven my own
daughter back. It's one sided. You
hug and hold and kiss goodbye,
but you really want to say "Stay,
don't change, don't grow away
from me." That was the anger
in us, the change we could not
stop, no matter what we said.
I did not want to know a word
he did not know, or read a book
he had not read. I did not want
to win an argument, though finally I did.
One night late I got the better of him.

Mom had even come down from
bed a couple times, to get us
to settle down and stop shouting.
Even my father knew, I think,
though he didn't say. Some technicality
and I had won. Or maybe I just
wore him down. "Well,
I'm going to bed," he said,
and started his climb up stairs.
And left me captain of the field.
The rest I don't remember.
Hard as it was to win, when I
had done it, what did it count?
We don't do that anymore. No
moment of contention arises.
I'm just glad to see him and he
me. We do our little dance
around each other, trying not to
make the other one ashamed of
us. Forty-five, nearly as bald
as he is, and with my beard,
looking as old, the joke's on me,
I guess, who wanted so much to
fight with his father. We are
home to our griefs now. You
may see him walking by,
slow, careful, he never wants to
pick an argument. He'll watch the
news, and shake his head, go in
and make dinner. He does things
carefully, to draw them out. Should
I have lost, I think, and would
that make him strong? Would that
be better than seeing him
so acquiescent now? Oh, he

could get furious in those days,
so mad it seemed to me
that all the anger of the world
was there, to keep me from
whatever I deserved. That
was his greatest love. To launch
me fit and sleek into the void,
thinking I'd earned my way
and knew a thing or two.
Somehow the path is cleared,
the father steps aside, the child
must want to go. That is the
way of the world. It's all mad.
It's like the trick in the movie,
the guy behind the door holds it
and bars it against all pounding.
Then when they throw their full
force against it he releases it,
and they rush through the house
and out the window and are gone.
That's how my father got rid of
me. One day I was on my
own, the wind whistling around
me. I didn't know a thing,
or where I was, or that I did
not know a thing. My father
let me win. All fathers do.
That is the trick of it.

Reciting "The Highwayman"

Miriam Gladding had the big leg,
and carried it around
like someone stepping in a garbage can
or wastebasket, and could not get it
off her foot. The nylon was
obscenely stretched, like a giant
water balloon, would it burst?—
or could we hear it slosh?
But when she spoke you thought
of what she said. You looked at
the leg, and maybe made a joke,
or maybe it seemed grotesque, whatever
that was, but when she spoke you
listened to the words. She
made you forget the leg. She
made you forget you were short
or tall, or had a wart, or cried
at night. She made you forget
you felt foolish or awkward—
just standing there in her dress,
with her leg below the knee
a gallon drum of slush, and
then she spoke. She made me forget
what century I lived in,
that I was ashamed I was
young, where she was old,
and well, where she was sick,
so when we opened up our
books one day I read "The Highwayman"
and I was he. She made me forget
that he dies. I read the

words, and they were words like hers,
convinced and organized.
And made me forget the
earth I was bounded to,
and I flew. Somehow I
told her I would memorize
the poem, and then some time
in class, all on my own, I
would recite it. It seemed
a natural thing, like walking
around with twenty pounds of
water in your leg, or coming
in to class and planting it,
like a tree in a pot,
and singing from a limb a
sweet sad song. I memorized
the poem. It happened overnight,
or in a glimpse. And then
she called on me. And I was
there, my hands behind my back,
my fingers in the chalk tray
on the wall, and looked around.
And then I said the poem.
It was like water flowing over
rocks. It had a song
and I knew every note. It was
a form of truth, a truth beyond
the truth of fact, and I
knew every word. It was
a dance, where never I had
danced, and yet I danced.
And came to the part about
the landlord's daughter in
the window and her lovely
hair, and looked around the

room at all the girls, and
though I had never loved,
or known love, I felt full
with her beauty, and their love,
and made even that convincing.
It was a great performance.
And came to the awful part
where she to save his life
pulls the trigger of the musket
leaning against her breast.
And dies. And though I had
never known death, I swallowed
and got through that, and
plunged on, to the incredible
part where he learns how she dies,
and what the gunshot meant,
and so rides back into a fusillade
and also dies. And so they
are together, where love can live
unvanquished by time. In a
place Miriam Gladding led me to,
the poetry of pain transcended.
I finished, and sat down, Miss
Gladding leading the applause.
And would always associate
beauty and poetry, of being
wholly lifted and transformed.
The next week, though I was
scrawny and had bad eyesight,
I did "Casey at the Bat"
for the kids of the seventh grade.

Photograph of My Mother Playing Pinochle

Mark is looking, the lucky one, over
his shoulder to berate me jokingly
for taking this, the thirty-third snapshot
of our rushed visit, or tenth in an hour,
when, setting the camera down I place it
near me as to have it ready, the way
a gunfighter positions his six-gun, handle
out in the leather holster, and then
surveys the room. Mark loves it, he
has a good hand, good meld, or maybe
lots of aces, or has decided to pass, and
can lean back in his chair, and smile
for the camera, because he is having a good
time, because he likes the fit of his clothes,
the lay of his mind, and being snowed
in, or knowing that, no matter what, no
matter how long it is he has to sit here
like this, listening to our jokes, we
will be going soon, the whole magic
show taken down, folded away back
in the car, and leave, push out onto the
hard pavement and head for home. Besides,
he loves us, and besides, he drinks a glass of
beer in public, in front of his Grandma,
out of the handmade stein she bought
him for Christmas, which means somehow
she understands, somehow, what it is
to be young, has not forgotten, having
had two sons, what a young man
likes, sometimes, to settle down with,
not a good book, not the nightly news

like she does, or a plate of stew
she made herself and never ceases to
remark how good it is, yum yum,
and lick up every drop of sauce, but
beer, filled to the brim, to throw
down gulps of, then, taking a breath,
letting the taste bloom on the tongue,
and then snap down his cards and
take his share of tricks, for always
there is more and more, a young man's
share, which each day grows until
someday perhaps he'll say "And now
the world?" viewed from a height
of aptitude or high accomplishment,
which is of course a hope we
reserve for young men. Behind
him, almost out of range of the
flashbulb that illuminates his
face, and brightens it, in shadows,
in the shadows where more and more
we consign the old, my
mother sits, holding herself up
in shadows. The bid has not passed
yet to her, or Mark has not yet played
his cards, or she has taken, the
way we do in company, a little time
to hold onto herself, to resume some
contact with that self that here,
each other day than this, a whole long
year, alone, surveys this miniscule
domain, which is the scope of that
long look she took once fifty
years ago, and, not seeing what it
came to, what it would come down
to, came on blindly into it,

the way Mark throws his jaw out
firmly in the flashing of the bulbs,
here in this place tonight. We
have no other choice. It is
a face of absolute misery, a
sudden sheared glimpse into the
void around which she with discipline
and care erects the facets of her life,
and I grab hold of the photograph,
and bring it nearer to my eyes,
with both the wonder and the
horror of it. Here is being
abandoned by a father who one day
walked out, and would not come
back, and did not even write, and
his own face which I saw once or
twice in old brown prints, cruel,
remote, a loveless face, who
walked out on his child, and her
being kicked around, unwanted, packed
in some apartment with uncles
and aunts, being trampled, made
obedient at best, to learn a few
hard lessons, then to emerge, to
escape, like a butterfly up from
the worm, a giddy flight into
a loveless marriage with my father
who, to this day cannot laugh,
and sit by a bed in a hospital
and watch a son die. Who knows
what mansion of misery haunts
the nights this child of my mother
walks in terrified, asking
"Is this my life? Is this what
my life will be?" Her face is

a face the masks have been
pulled from, the way in photographs
catching a notch in the sequence
of images which comprise the
animated face we give the world,
one frame sticks, one naked slice
across the breadth of everything,
the skull beneath the flesh,
the space inside the skull, where,
for everything we know of our desires,
a piece of gravel rattles as we
pick it up out of the dirt. She
holds her hand of cards in front of
her, holding it with both her
hands, like it is all there is,
a few more tricks to play, and
then she is done, who never once
had a real hand, anything with
winners she could play, win with,
or throw down laughing. No,
she must play with these, no
points, no power, no length,
nothing to answer with, nothing
to flash around or brag about,
just going through the motions,
as all around her all the rest
of them are— what?— are young,
are thin, are smart, are rich,
who sleep in late, who never have
to work, who throw their money down
and never care, or it fly
out the window, never mind,
and laugh, because there is no
joke on them, not yet.
Her mouth is open, her teeth

show, it looks as if she is
straining not to cry out,
not to condemn life, her face
flushed in the shadows, steeped
in the heat of hurt,
or straining to conceal herself
from everyone, and from
herself, from herself the most.
We are what we believe
we are. We sleep at night for
having made whatever we can make
and call the measure of an effort.
It has been a long day for her.
There have been, in short, many
setbacks and humiliations.
Now, dinner over, gathered around
her her family she never sees,
she will relax with cards,
and drink a glass of wine,
and watch her grandson flash his
confidence around until the
very night is gone. And each
goes off, alone, as she is,
alone, and the house goes quiet
like any other house,
as outside snow falls on the
parking lot.

What It Was

for John Brehm

John says his friend says
"You have a fish, but it
would be better if
it were a toad, or bird."
And John says "No, it was
a fish, that's what it was."
His friend says "But that's
Art, and Art can be most
anything it wants." But John
says "No, it was a fish."
The poem is in the thing
itself. We look to see
just what it is precisely.
"It's like Michelangelo, who
dug into the rock to free
the forms inside." The
poetry is there, a living
presence in the world.
All we have to do is find
it. That's why facts are
so important, that's why
what it was is just the
place to start.

So too there is the
fact of the poem.
The poem itself is fact,
the word we choose to
be the first, and then the

next, the word we choose
to be the next. Pretty
soon you have a line or
two, which marks the
place the poem begins.
"It's like Woodstock. They
didn't start the film when
Hendrix sang, or when the
first act came out.
They built the stage up
out of the dirt and the
mud. They went back
even earlier, a bird on
a limb of a tree,
some wind in the grass."
When does the film begin?
You settle in your seat, you
spill your popcorn, you remove
your husband's coat. Someone
is nailing boards in the rain.
Is this the music of The
Grateful Dead? Are they in
the movie? You don't know
yet. Maybe this film is about
the making of "Woodstock."
Or about the boys who built
the stage, not the stage at
Woodstock, but all the barns
they practiced on. Here is
Jimi at eleven. He had
a choice between the hammer
and the guitar. He chose the
guitar whereas his father chose
the hammer. And might be
alive now if he'd chosen

different. So too the
poem. We go back before
now. There is a yesterday
the fish was small. Out
of an egg it hatched,
and spun around all tail
in a drop of water.
It got dizzy spinning.
Went down and hugged
the bottom. It liked
the dark. Learned to eat
grubs and small dark worms.
It liked the taste. It
could not help itself.
And when it rained it
got excited. Anything
with water. Water and then
more of it. The fish
had many fears, but
not of water. Men fear
water and respect the fish.
Along came John. He was
fishing. He cast out
into the green water.
What's that? A tug on his
line? This is how a
fish makes a house call.
This is how a fish
stops a train. It
pulls on the line.
John's father taught him
how. He thought it
was important. His
father did not know about
poems, how poems would

be more important than
fish. "You've caught a
fish," John's father said.
That's what it was.
John's friend says, "I
thought it was a bird
you caught?"

When Barb and I went
to the movies to see
"Woodstock," my Grandma
Bradshaw went with us.
I can't remember why.
Perhaps she had nothing
to do. Here was a woman
over sixty who didn't like
music and had no education,
who worked in a lampshade
factory, and then made
bathing caps. She had one
friend in all the world.
One daughter. Each year
she came to visit us, a long
day on the train. We
went to the theatre.
I sat and looked at people
like myself, young men
in beards and long hair,
wearing jeans. Between
the seat my Grandma sat
in and the screen a
chasm opened.
She sat there the whole
time. When Country Joe
came out, along with

The Fish, and yelled out
"Fuck," my Grandma showed
she had not gone to sleep.
Each time he said the
word her head flew back.
She never left. She
sat there the whole
time. Afterwards,
I asked her what she
thought. She said she
enjoyed herself.

How did she get like she
was? When did the poem
of her life begin?
What drop of water did
she emerge from, spinning,
what dark did she go to
sleep in, growing into
herself?
So, someone says to
me, "Your grandma,
watching 'Woodstock,'
have her— like— walk on
wires over the chasm. Have
her dance off towards the
screen. She loved you!
She stayed. She did it
for you." I know, I
say. She loved me,
and her head flew back.

How I Got My Name

I don't know. No one told me.
Nor did I ask. In a book, perhaps?
My parents went through it, on
a Sunday afternoon. The last time
they did a thing both shared
in equally. What goes with
Kuzma? Who do we have
already? Or some such question.
Stew was bubbling in a pot. My
mother had me neatly tucked
inside. I had not yet begun to
climb the walls. Or keep them
up all night, afraid of the dark.
Or run a fever, bring the doctor
out at 10 p.m., with his black
bag. Later I would look at
it and say, "Is this what I am?"
Is this my father driving off
to work, who might have gone
anywhere, and never told about
it. But come back home again,
and pull in the driveway. Some
secret life he had, which bought
the food, and mother did the
wash, then went to work. I
knew no other Gregs, no other
Kuzmas. Two strange names
to be embarrassed by. Were my
parents good with words? My
father never talked, except to
prove to me I was learning a

lesson. The early bird, for instance,
whom I never saw, sleeping in,
while the bird got the worm.
But why would I want a worm,
I thought. What's the point of
getting up? Or kindness and
weakness, about not getting the
two mixed up. "Don't confuse,"
my father said, "Kindness and
weakness." Meaning, I suppose,
he was kind, not weak, or if I
continued to push against him
we would "get down to brass
tacks." My mother never stopped
talking. And would have talked
to me whatever I was called.
I was just there, "part and
parcel" of the world, came
home, threw my books on the
counter, collapsed in a chair.
The day was too long. I hated
being called on. Hated waiting,
day after day, until, at last,
again, I heard my name.
It hung in the air like
something ugly and alive.
"Gregory Kuzma," Mrs. Hawks
would say. No one wanted it, no
one stood to claim it. So at
last, reluctantly, blushing,
trying to hide my face, I
acknowledged the crime. How
could you like a name nobody
but some strangers had, who
laughed uproariously, or sat in

sullen quiet all through dinner.
I was torn between being
bold and being meek. Don't
confuse boldness with meekness,
my father never said. Your
mother's bold, while I am meek.
"And never the twain
shall meet." They meet in
me. To say or not to say?
That is the question. And sat
there with the answer like a
bomb about to go off. Was
it correct? How come nobody
knew but me? And sat in
guilty and embarrassed silence.
Embarrassed to know. Embarrassed
not to know. What had I done
with myself? Embarrassed
to be. In gym class embarrassed
when we counted off. Was
I to be a one, a two, a three?
Or four? Then split our ranks,
while I looked down the row
to see the faces of the other
"ones." I hated being defined.
I did not want to be in
class. I hated my shorts.
I hated my skinny legs. I
did not want to see my legs
were skinny. I did not
want to wait while others
talked. Hated the silence that
my mother made my father
keep, until, in resignation,
and revenge, he would not speak

at all. But got up from the
table, pushed his chair back,
and left. Later we'd be
hearing his saw slicing wood,
or some pounding. Meaning
he was finally relaxed.
Embarrassed not to know the
right way to file a piece of
wood, or how to put a counter
sink in wood, for the head of
the screw. Embarrassed not to
care. But just as sure I
did not want to know. "Don't
take me with you, and don't
leave me home," my father said.
Referring to his mother's favorite
words. By ten I think I was
ready to leave. I had had
enough. I was tired of my
face getting hot every time
I felt I ought to know or could
not know, every time I tried
and failed, or won the
admiration of the teacher.
Proud, I blushed, for caring so
much, for thinking I could win
my way beyond the hurt.
It would not have mattered
what my name was. I was
at odds with life. I was
born in a wrong time.
Whatever it was I disapproved
of it. And needed something
to do where I could transform
the world. Each day it shook

me with its cruel inadequacies.
The boy who was too fat, my
friend, and many laughed. The
boy who was too strong, and
frightened me. The boy who
screamed "Fuck" in my face,
and said, "Go home and ask your
mother what it means." And had
to go to my room, as if I
had done something bad,
and wait for my father.
The one time it wasn't a
lesson. He could see I
had nothing at all to do
with it. He could see
how much I suffered
for having been born with
two legs. Who saw me run,
not fast enough, and wag
my tongue, not smart
enough. You could never be
enough. I knew that right
away. My mother must have
taught me on her knee,
and bounced me there until
I wanted more, and liked it,
and so wanted more.
And then she stopped, to
invest in me a definition
of value. More of what
we're used to, that's what
we want. And so became
a poet of embarrassments.
Each day to suffer the world's
hurts, each night like my

father, sneaking home under
cover of darkness, in the
twilight, to crawl my belly
up the stairs, and lie there
stricken, about to expire.
Only the words I said
alone in my room restored
me. Changing the names.
Changing the time to suit
me. Making the hero look
like me. "And then he got
the girl." Not knowing what
to do with her. Words I
pored over in the dark.
All the things that I had
meant to say, or would have
said, had not my face been
red. I wrote to keep from
being red. New versions
of old sad things. Where
the compromised world
no longer has to shudder
and walk away, astonished,
but can lift itself, where
I can lift myself, and sing.
Poetry came out of shame.
Poetry came out of pain.
To bounce back from defeat
into a poem. It's true, I am
a fool, or I was wrong, or
I was slow, or I said something
bad, but please forgive me
now, here is my poem.
Apologies to the world.
Apologies for the world,

and so on. The words gushed
forth. All the years of being
lectured to, or having to sit
in class and speak only
when spoken to. "Children
should be seen and not heard,"
my mother said. But then
when speaking, everybody laughed
to watch his face get red.
Even in the dark sometimes
writing the poem, my heart would
pound. The words ran forth
like children running home,
a hail of the world's snowballs
over them. Here was where
the bully could not reach.
And she who made me shy
for all the beauty of her face,
I could love without apology.
And so I came to find a way
to love the world and to
forgive my life. I would
stay up nights, after the day
had stumbled to some crude
completion, accidentally
crushing the cat, accidentally
making the tire flat, or
sweating at the party through
my shirt, and write another
chapter of the world's story,
this time perfected, this
time every issue clarified,
defined and unambiguous.
And at the bottom of each
page I wrote my name.

Greg Kuzma, poet of the
world's deficiencies,
poet of the world's inadequacies,
freak of nature, unaccommodated
one, restless soul, the night
sky star that never sleeps
but shines even against the sun's
fury, poet of his father's angry
silence and his mother's gab.
East met west in my name. North
south, night day, for whatever
reconciliation there might be,
and struggled off to sleep,
to wake up for another dawn,
where it would all start up again,
and we are either lost or found.

Grandma

It was the purest love—
what I felt for her. And have
not written of it, for fear
the words betray us, as words do.
And no accounting will add up to
the sum of its wealth.
But far in excess, as God so loved
the world in all its vast abundance
we are lost in. It was like that,
endless and vast, the tide come
in a thousand miles, the air
at fifteen thousand feet, the
view over the pole. Yet
centered in homey things,
small miracles— as if to belie
our range and reach— cookies
out of the oven come melting
and cooling at once, on the
countertop— to float
on a sheet of waxed paper,
leaving their imprint— my
home base back from forays
into happenstance. She lived
with us for a while, I can't
remember well, while Mom
worked. Became synonymous,
as it were, with the house itself—
sitting in a chair, sewing, one
might ask what could be wrong?—
there could be nothing wrong—
and go to sit on her lap, reach

out my hand to paddle gently
the dewlap flesh hung down
from her upper arm. She was
all gentleness— too passive
for the world's insistent stare—
I learned later, from others, as
they told me, and never said No
to me as I remember, and would
do anything I asked, without
thinking, without compunction.
Such love doubles and magnifies.
That which is without reservation
knows no argument, cannot be
convinced or dissuaded, but
rises full always, like a spring up
out of the ground, nor can we
put our hands on it to keep it
down, but splashes our face—
our hands not able to hold it—
dance in its waters— until we
bend to drink and take that
sweetness— as if from the
earth's lips. We could not be
left alone together— we could
not be trusted— for what brand
of mischief we would make—
would take all the pots and
pans out of the cupboards
and pound on them with
wooden spoons— each had
a tin tone like a drum— and
dent the bottoms sometimes—
then shove the telltale pots
back in, deep in the back, before
Mom got home. Or tip the

chairs down sideways on the
floor, and drape the blankets
over them— to make my
"mousey house"— and though
she was old, she must have
been fifty then at least— would
crawl in with me under there—
the light diffuse, and came through
an orange glow, warm and soft
as sleep. She had no policies
or programs, no laws or rules,
was always open to experience,
yet frightened too, a bit shy—
I saw that maybe once or twice—
but no opinions, really, anything
was what it was— she'd take
it out and look at it, nor make
a judgment. On her the world
would write its terrible lessons—
her husband left her early, after
one child, ran off with a woman,
but nothing ever registered,
she was like water written on
by wind— soft, pliable, no
mind of its own, and could get
whipped up sometimes— mother
could make her swear, in sympathy
for some anger mother felt—
then the feeling passed, the
surface untroubled again, the
eyes open and trusting once
more. It was funny to watch her—
like a child, to mirror or echo the
mood, originating none herself,
and if the people with her

laughed or cried, you'd turn
to her and she'd be crying
too— like a baby in a room of
shouters, becoming agitated
too, and shake its little hands
in front of its face, until we
soothed it with our whispers.
Was I myself her kind?— fragile,
gentle, and without design?
The two of us gone naked
in the world. She was a
famous smoker. She smoked
a lot, and had an amazing habit.
All my life of smoking, and
being with smokers, I've
never seen the likes of this.
The ash on her cigarette
would get immensely long.
I mean it would comprise nearly
the whole thing. I forget her
brand. We would be talking,
or doing something, and then
I'd notice her ash— bent over
from its own weight, drooping
like a waving crinoid stem
in ancient seas, or witch nose
of a wise old woman— the
cigarette hung from her lips,
or held in one hand, the other
cupped beneath it like an ashtray.
"Grandma," I'd yell at her—
"Your cigarette!" Then she
would laugh, and start to cough,
laughing and coughing,
showing her long teeth. I

found her beautiful, flawless,
perfect in every way. She had
a way about her— that when she
was with me we needed no one
else. And visited her in Whitestone
once, at her house— on a trip where
I was to visit Toby, and go to
The City. I went to New York
instead with Grandma. It was
like the old days, riding the bus
on the Island, then the subway
over. We went to Macy's
of course— her favorite store,
and didn't buy a thing. But
then hit the deli for lunch.
I remember her big dark bag,
smelling of chocolates and
cigarettes, and watched her
take the roll of money out, it
wasn't much, and buy us
our favorite, pastrami on rye,
with Thousand Island dressing.
She bought me my first car.
It's amazing. I cry when I
think of it. Making lampshades
or bathing caps, putting her
money into bonds— twenty
years later she passed on to
me $800. It was a red MG,
extravagant and glamorous,
like she never was. I took
her for a ride that year when
she came to visit, sitting beside
me, the top down, a red scarf
or *babushka* on her head.

We drove, like I could make
her young, or drive so fast
we might go back in time,
to feel what I felt, or a little
scared perhaps, but laughing
all the way. She was never
old and mean, the way some
people get, angry at the young
for being young, jealous of them,
but treated me as if we were
the same, nor could I wrong
her. I would write to her all
the years at college. And work
hard at things she never
understood. Would study hard
for six hours, copy all the day's
notes in each separate folder,
then, to treat myself, re-imagine
my life as it might be told to her.
And she would answer in a
week or so, and folded in
among the two sheets of
her letter, a five dollar bill!
So is compassion born, even
in the young and selfish. It
is the work of love, to teach us
all things. Without it we are
monsters. Weak as she was—
and there are those who call
her so— I had rather be alone
with her than anyone. She was
the perfect companion. Like a
mirror or an echo, or a shadow,
so in parallel to everything you
did, that you could see your

very self, as in a novel or a
movie, no shock of disapproval
ever marked her face. She
had nothing. She had a bed,
which later I gave away. She
had a chair or two, and lived
in an apartment with another
woman. But I did not notice
her poverty. We were together,
that was what mattered. Her
favorite card game was canasta.
We would play for hours.
I cannot remember who won—
or she was the first person
I wanted to win besides myself.
Nor can I remember the rules.
I never played with anyone but
her. Maybe we even made up
our own rules— to laugh the
whole time till we cried.
Beyond us the mad exacting world
punished both good and bad,
even the ironists— it punished
both Mom and Dad— but spared
us as if by magic— love shielded us,
as whosoever is of true heart
cannot be harmed. So Jesus
taught, and Grandma too, my
private tutor. At her right
hand may I live out my days.
She lives still in my forgiveness.
Hurt, punished at last, in the
wild unruly wind beyond reach
of her love, no matter, I am
with her still. She is what lives

in everyone whom I am drawn to,
some essential self astonished
as its own joy— laughing—
coughing— and I can laugh, and
last night hugged Rodney Jones—
Imagine that! — though he had
angered me— forgetting— forgiving—
I was hugging her— or she was
hugging him. No corruption
can obtain over her for long
its advantage. Even in my
darkest hour she resided,
somewhere within me, bitter
as I was, her face brightened
in mine and I was spared.
Innocent, without guile,
with never a thought for herself
or what she might get, without
bitterness, hers was an eloquent
life— and I the only one escaped
to tell thee. Our visits were few,
our time together brief. Yet
it was enough. So in tight pockets
of the secret self her spirit resides,
even in the dark or darkest time,
grace in a gesture or a word,
keeping faith. She would call
me Gregalee. The only one to
ever call me that. A sort of
magic name— like something
out of a fairy tale, my secret name.
"Gregalee," she'd say, and say
it sweetly like bird song. She
was not asking anything, merely
naming me among the world's

endless roll call of its billion names,
like bird song, which names both
namer and named, there is such
love in it. Our greatest thing of all
was New Year's Eve. Tradition
from the dawn of time. There are
photos of me in slipper socks,
and three feet tall, helping Grandma
with the snacks. She called them
our "goodies"— and smacked
her lips, leaning over a tray of
crackers with sardines, each
cracker with its own sardine,
to make them all look more
presentable. Once begun like
this in innocence, we could not
stop, like raising the retarded
child, almost invisible among
the six-year-olds, but as he
aged, more obviously in arrears,
until at twenty, bloated in short
pants, monstrous and sad, to
stand there holding Mommy's hand.
It was like that with Grandma.
I caught her on some giant
plateau, done with whatever
climbing she would do, 50
and 55 and 60, resigned perhaps
that she would not remarry,
friendless except for Mrs. Dragon,
a brother and sister she hardly
saw, when New Year's Eve
came round, she had, of course,
no plans, no invitations to go
out. But I was twelve, and then

fourteen, and then sixteen, and
had a girl or two. No matter.
We had our tradition. Each
year she'd come at Christmas
for the Holidays, and we would
do our New Year's Eve together.
At first she managed all the
work herself, but older, I would
help her. We were big on
sardines and anchovies— why
I never knew— I haven't eaten
an anchovy since, cream cheese
on crackers and we would make
enough for a small army. I
have these photographs of
Grandma sitting by a TV tray,
staring at a plate of crackers
we'd prepared— her whole
attention focused on the plate.
And would sit there the whole
night after Mom and Dad
went out, and watch TV,
and eat our goodies. And
watch the shining ball come
down the pole in Times Square
while Guy Lombardo played
the famous song. I can't
recall a thing we talked about—
but was synonymous with
consciousness itself— whatever
that we did was like the air we
breathed— I can't recall
a single breath I took in all
those years— yet I am here and
did not fail to breathe. So is

love essential and invisible—
noticed only in its absence.
Then will we gasp and grab
ourselves in that dying—
who never knew what air
we breathed or water that
we drank. Of her am I made.
Water and breath. Grandma
my source and wellspring
in the world. Presiding spirit,
Grandma Bradshaw. Let me
name her now in turn, let me
say her pretty name— Estelle—
Estelle Bradshaw.

Reading Student Poems

Nearly dead from reading the poems
I try to get up, but can't. My legs
are numb. Outside the night is cold.
I dream of my escape into Canada,
to sit in a bar all day and drink beer.
I would not even want to fuck
the girls, just sit and drink and
read the papers. Or I could slit
my wrists. There is the poetry of how
the blood comes, reckless, out of the
wound. The body goes on thinking
that its tubes are all intact, the
heart does not revise itself, does
not falter. Poetry should be like that,
drawing the knife over the pale wrist,
or setting out at dawn, heading north,
leaving it all behind. Instead,
I go on sitting here. It is the end
of the twentieth century. Children
are coming along the lonely road of
life. They scribble on the backs
of paper bags their love songs
to the world. I read them and I weep.
I correct their grammar. I correct
their spelling. I look at a phrase,
I look at it, I cock my head to the side,
like Starbright used to do in wind,
my dog who died, and try it that way.
I say the words aloud. Here are
the words I used to use to tell the
story of the brother who died. Here

is the wind that blew around the house
the night the words came through the phone
to tell the truth of how he was no more.
My father said exactly, "He didn't
make it." My student writes exactly
in "Buena Bulldogs": "Mother, aunt,
little brother, girlfriend,/ four
fatalities./ Drunken Driver 502,/
escaped with minor injuries." My head
reels reading the words. I put on my
brother's blood, I think of him, the
drunken driver who died. If thirteen
years connect the events, there is a
bridge of words. Can we sort out what
we know? I lived beyond the stranglehold
of grief, to be here tonight, to read
these words. My "little brother" is dead.
I marvel at how kind the poem is, not
to hate the reader for not caring, for
coming in off the streets, being bored.
What will I say tomorrow in class?
Dear Lord of Poetry, give me an eloquent
day. Let my tongue heal over
the wounds of the words. There is
this faith we have, that in the setting
down on paper, some reality is forged.
We drift, we knock about, we laugh, we
suffer. Then, with a pen, we scribble
out some sort of mooring in the storm.
Tonight it's being strong, not bursting
into tears. A harmless looking page,
a poem about a night of basketball,
and then the deaths. Can I feel the pain
of he who wrote the words? Do I feel
my own thirteen years later? No, I would

get away. I would run through flowers,
scaring the bees. Or sit and drink coffee
all day. Tired, worn out with longing,
I would sit in a movie house and eat
popcorn. Well, it doesn't matter.
If I won't read his poem in class,
he can bash his car into a tree, or
spend a sleepless night. Having suffered
so much, what can someone's caring matter?
If I fail, at least I tried. And so
on. Bearing my heart away. They are all
not like this. Some are dumb. Some mad
virus infects the lines, some insane
virus of a rhyme distorts the smooth
completion of the words. You writhe
reading the words. And what is the poem
about? It's hard to say. And could it
be improved fifteen percent?
That is the task at hand. Writing
now to write again tomorrow. Not
to be done, not to blaze out in a
blaze of glory, not to say words
beyond pain, but to progress a little
like a knife sawing the skin. Soon
we will have a full bloom of the blood.
And if I kill myself, will it stop?
My blood will pump a little lake
beside my chair. Next day, in class,
they'll have another poet holding forth.
Beauty must be served. The young
must have their say, the meek shall inherit.
We must start all over again with
each new generation. No, that is
a cliché…No, that is too private.
Yes, you show an interest in the

world. And so on, a hundred
different variations on failure.
We can live, we can break hearts,
we have our numbers on file at
the IRS, on the street a reporter
stops us for an interview, the cold
instructs our hands to hide within our
coat. We are alive! What does it
matter if we cannot say it gracefully?
I am alive, I came, I made my little
song. Each semester I have three
classes. The kids come in cold
from high school. Somewhere in
the dim and distant past some lady
in a hairnet read them poems.
They hated them. They are prepared
to hate this too. School is boring,
someone says. And means it. Oh
the infinite capacity to be bored.
If it is not for me the bird sings
on the branch then I am bored. The
poem about the dead family is boring.
The poem where Richard Blessing tells
the story of his cancer. No, it is
not like that. We are of good will.
We want to see the rivers flowing
on the moon. We want to see the rivers
flowing as they used to flow. We
want to sit around the table listening
to others talk. Today we have the poem
about addiction. We asked— Do you
think it should be in the first person?
Are you yourself an addict? We try to
praise the challenges of that. To
extend our sympathies. We're rich,

we're young, but let's today pretend
we are sick and old. A bottle sits
on our shoulder like a savage bird.
We drink from it each night, it pecks
our eyes out. Someone says, I think
the poem should be more violent.
I have a friend who broke his ankle.
Drunk, he discovered it, and jumped
up and down to make it worse. But
Terri says, the poet— "No, she is not
like that. She is small and cute and
quiet and sips her drink and sips so
quietly until she falls over." Canada
beckons. I am starting the car.
I have my sleeping bag and gear,
my maps, my fishing pole. To sneak
across the border at midnight,
chased by the poem police.
I see the lonely stars over Canada.
By them I will plot my way.
And come to a cabin deep
in the woods, a stack of firewood,
an axe, perhaps a faithful dog.
I will adopt a wolf, rejected from the
pack. Nights he will curl by my feet.
No, I will bring him with me
into the bed. He will teach me
to eat raw fish and mice. Things
taken on the run. The only poetry
will be the creek calling out
as it tickles its belly over the
stones. No, I will never leave.
My schedule is a sacred pledge.
I have made a pact with them,
the young, to listen to their cries

All That Is Not Given Is Lost

forever. It is midnight on the
blank white sheet. From deep
inside them secret thoughts are
marshaling themselves. Secret armies
in the service of the truth are rising.
They have crossed the river into
tomorrow. Amidst a million lies
the truth of the poem will be heard.
The storm of the poem comes, that is
its dust. That is the sound
of its feet in the clamor of typewriter
keys. He hands me a stack of pages,
clipped with a large silver clip.
He says, I am a fiction writer, but
lately, for a particular class whose
name I will not say, I've been writing
poems. Yes, I will take them, I say.
I take the sacred pages in my hand,
pretend the weight is killing me,
that I cannot lift the weight of the
stack. We laugh. Later, reading,
I come across the poem about the kid
putting his head on the Xerox. It
is the greatest thing. Describing
perfectly the rack sliding through,
the hum, the brilliant square
of light, his yellow eyelids
closed against it. And then
what monstrous picture is this,
a face against the blacks of Hell?
A view of the stolen soul. Or,
in his best image, his face
beneath the ice, holding his breath,
pressed there, flattened.
There is no end. There will not

be an end. We go on,
we go on. We stop. We cannot
go on. It is all too much, it
is all too new, it is all too
joyous a thing. So, what do you
do in class?— someone asks. She
fidgets. She doesn't know. You
do what you can, I tell her. You try
to be as alive as you can. And if
you have nothing to say, you let
the others talk. There is an
innate genius in the language.
No one owns it. It belongs to
the world, to language itself.
It sings of itself even when
we're not there to hear it.
We keep faith with it if we can.
We help others to keep faith.
My legs are sore now, numb
from sitting. I am coming
awake in a room where I sat
but never was. My body was there,
but I was out traveling, over
the hills of poems. The wolf led
me. The kid with his Xerox machine.
He leads it along on a leash, and
now and then we take another picture
of a tree, a mountain range, a
snowbank under clouds. Here are
the dead uprisen, the ones killed
by the drunk. Their lives ripped
from them in a cruelty which we
will not forget. Still, they are
standing with their poet. His
duty is to keep them fresh in

memory. Here is my brother I could
not save, saved in a poem. You
would not know he lived at all
except for my words. They are
all here, count them. Your father
is here, and your mother also.
Your sons and your daughters are here,
or will come here. The dog that ran
away, the dog that was run over by
the car that did not stop, the
driver looking back, forgetting,
writing his poem to speed. Here
is the rain after a long day,
healing the thirst of the ground.
Here is the wind come in around
the house now where you sit.
It rustles the curtains. Now
longing fills you, a dream of a
happy time. You are a child again,
alive in the spring. Your grandmother,
the one who died last year, and
would not be consoled, who stared
at the wall three years, was young
then. She calls you from the window
of the house. Your name on the tongue
of the world, in the world's mouth.
You will remember that. That's
what your poem will recall.
And so you set your hand to paper.

Burning the Candle at Both Ends

Whenever I would get out of hand,
which is a metaphor he did not use,
my father said to me, how I was
doing it, "burning the candle at both
ends," and maybe added "boy," to
finish it. I can still hear him.
Like all his famous sayings it was
physical, something to see or touch.
He might have said— and will forgive me
from this vantage here beyond the grave,
"You're overdoing it," or you are
overcommitted— perhaps that you have
"taken on" too much. I'm stretching
now for something without cargo
or wheels or skin to rub against,
or hot breath down our necks,
but here, where writing "taken on,"
I see in keeping with his thought
a large sailing vessel taking on a
stream of gold grain in its hold,
or worse, sinking, taking on the
full weight of the sea, a huge roll
of green water rushing in over
the side— to signal the disaster
as intended, which marked the doom
of my plans, or cast a shadow on the
ground I stood on. Everything he
said had something of the earth in
it, and he was very fond of animals,
horses especially, perhaps because
his father used them in those early

years. Poppa worked horses, and
kept them in the barns out back,
where as a child I'd gone and stood
amidst the grease and crank case oil
spilled on the floor. There was no
smell of horses, but there must have
been, blended with stuck paint in
old brushes, linseed oil in jars,
with a few dead moths floating on
top, like flies in amber. The
past preserved, held in suspension,
before time eats of it and we are
gone. And watched time comb his
hair down off his head till he was
young no more. And had seen his
father shrink down into the man I
knew, the passion wrung from him
like water out of a towel. In
those last years Poppa seemed inert.
What of the father of my father—
I who am haunted so by mine— haunted
him?— and hurt him into poetry as
Auden says it must. Every third
expression has a horse in it,
looking a gift horse in the mouth,
a horse of a different color, or
the parable of the nail in the shoe,
which loosens and the world shudders,
outward in rings of greater and greater
consequence, sweeping us all along
and away. Or "irons in the fire"—
which might be branding irons, and
beyond, again, the horse as ultimate
object. Then to link up sayings by
their themes— how many promoting

the same position, the same degree of
caution or respect for property and
work and time and distance— how much
one could be expected to do— which
maybe was his last defense against my
burgeoning ambitions. No, he could not
go fishing, but had these other pools
to study, to stare into, his windows
of a Saturday, and rubbed the fishy
streaks quite out of them. We lived
in the city. Cars stormed behind
our house in a river of noise and grime,
their horses screaming underneath their
hoods— these horses with us still.
How many untold millions lived and died
in their shadows? Or came to be born
from the buggy trot of the country
doctor on his stops, delivering the
child at midnight in the snows, his
horse out steaming in the barn, its face
in oats. It was the same for candles.
We never used them. Old lamps instead
surrounded me, that had held wicks
to bring the oil up out of the reservoir,
and looked so pretty in the grace of
their lost forms. They were all converted.
Father would get them at the antique
stores, bring them home and wire them,
snake the cord up through and twist the
socket on, until you could not see
what they had been before, the logic
of their argument, form without function,
form as beauty only, beauty without
urgency. Candles we used for that rare
dinner, maybe at Christmas, Mother and

Father done with romance by the time I
stirred and walked abroad on two legs,
tipping over teacups on the knickknack
shelf. Candles like horses, remnants
from a bygone age, to drip down the
witch's skull in the dismal dungeon in
"Snow White," or in some Dumas novel I
was plowing through, dripping candles,
plunging necklines, flashing swordplay
down the banisters. Like everything
he put his mind to, it was loss he found,
the famous bottle of the pessimist always
half empty, no matter how fine the wine.
Not its light to draw us near in deep
confessionary talk, or flutter like the
heart's elusive heat, to make us hold
it gentle in some long embrace, but
time's cruel progress down the candle
stem, each moment drawn up out of a
fixed reserve, no more obtaining, no
image of the well to which, insatiable,
the thirsty come, and draw the water up
in sweet replenishment, then to refill
itself anew. In the candle was the
conscience of the man, America with all its
eastern trees cut down, the gray edge
of the plague of progress running westward
like wildfire, burning it all. I often
wonder what had happened to him, what had
so scorched his mind, and left him limping,
saving and skimping against what vast
disaster still to come— as he prepared,
it seemed, always for another day,
storing up vast quantities of things,
but never spending in the present tense.

In basement storage rooms he'd stack
the beer cans high, case after case,
box after box of motor oil, and in his
desk drawers in his bedroom, thousands of
rounds of ammunition— against what foe?
Out of what hunger to stalk the last
polar bear, and shoot it for its tongue?
One of his favorite stories was the demise
of the passenger pigeon. He told it often,
always with the same grim humor. How
they had once darkened the skies, and
Audubon, who stood in a grove in Illinois,
and the flock came towards him and flew
above his head solid for three hours.
How men would go and shoot them till they
filled the wagons up, profligate nature,
profligate hunger— until they shot the
last one sitting on its shrub in Kansas.
There could never be enough, apparently.
You never could be sure enough. Nor all
mad nature give us certainty. And the
last one sat in its shrub in Kansas, with
its tiny wavering flame, alone against
the dark, and then snuffed out forever.
He could not abide my wastefulness.
To waste my laughter on the wind,
or sheets of paper in the typewriter,
writing a scrap or two of nonsense,
then another sheet. I collected records,
45s, would play them over and over,
watching them spin, trying to read the
label in the blur, beautiful colors,
or hear the dirty words in "Quarter to
Three"— to saturate my mind with them
until I wore them out— what?— two weeks

later, and then bought another, the new
one canceling the last, how one thing
drives another out, or things grow stale
with us, the way I've never worn out Barb,
but see new depths of beauty there.
Beside me in my vision of the record listener,
the stack of worn out records rises
skywards like a stack of slugs or slagheap
spoilbank Wendell Berry talks of in his
essays, of the Eastern and the Western
coal fields of Kentucky. Or like some
candle rising from the floor beside me,
only the one on top, the one still
spinning on the turntable, burning in
its music. To use the earth, use up
the earth, as we have done, are doing,
and will do, in every conjugation of
its ruin and ours. I was his future there
beside him, like twin candles blazing,
or two ends of the same, and slept
upon the floors he swept, and ate
the very food he cooked, and yet his
enemy in youth's mad buoyancy, to doom
him somewhere down the road. Each day
his candle burned down further, while
I danced to my crazed music as the
records spun their web of fire, and
was myself the flame upon his wick and
wax, burning up his life. And how he
shrunk down further every year, his
patience wearing thin for all my
trespasses, bending to pick up messes
I'd made, the sawdust scattered of my
woodwork escapades, his files no longer
sorted by size or grade, his tools far-flung

across the growing junkyard of the world.
How he would burn to see the damage done,
a whole shelf of his jars with lids
punched through, my butterflies gasping
inside, the flare-ups of their wings
fading, or colors dimming in the
speckles of the trout, aground on the
bank of the stream. One candle was
enough, for sure, and we should use
it sparingly he said, for the life thrust
in it, life bearing light and heat, ere we
are dead and cold. But what if we
burn from both ends at once? What
fool would do that? Double light and
double heat but half the time. What
candleholder did they make for that?
I can think of none, to turn the candle
on its side, except his bench vise in the
cellar would be such a holder. So
I lived my life beneath his chilly gaze
and discipline, extravagant joy, the
rampage of my breath against the cage's
bars, my father's disapproval my jailer.
Using his wood one night around his fire,
stacking it on, beyond the two small
Scrooge logs he placed there when he went
to bed— a nice discreet fire— Barb and
I aflame in the wine, talking, smoking,
piling the wood high up, flames leaping
towards the stars, expressive of our
very souls, jumping and snapping in our
throats. Then went to bed to lie there
and to hear someone, Dad or Bill, spraying
the fire out, the hissing of the quick
expiring coals. The only times I've ever

loved my life were when I burned in my
full fury, not even sure if anything were
saved into the next moment, like now,
teetering on this edge of consciousness,
burning my mind up out of the stored wax
of memory for the sheer joy of the telling.
What will I store against some future dark,
I ask, in his words, burning my candle
at both ends, my two ends of my lines
a ragged uncertain mark, and nothing
spared to shore against the probable
reception of the reader, cold. When he
died we had the task of going to his
house to clear it out. You can imagine
what it looked like. Everything he'd
ever owned was there, and twenty versions
of each thing. In his closet, pants
he had not worn for thirty years hung neat
and pressed, battalions of his shirts. The
whole weight of his life hung there,
like unburned candles. I tried his shoes
on— some metaphor in that?— which did not
fit, then put his jackets on, but
not my style. And while I anguished over
everything, in that cave of my remorse,
just punishment for a misspent youth,
Barb took the whole full closet and tossed
it in a dumpster at the Salvation Army—
to show me how to set myself on fire
for the work ahead. There were dark places
in that house, rooms I had not visited in
years, the ghost of my brother in a room
we could not get enough light into. To
ask for every light to keep the dark back,
every candle from its both ends burning,

and set the drapes on fire keeping out
the sun, and all the furniture we could not
use tossed on, and hauled his books off
to the library. Six weeks later we had
the auction. It came on the day of my
birth, July 14, and sent the notices around,
and cars came in from fifty miles away
to bring joy to that house and yard.
Locks he had kept shut on his doors flew
open to admit the strangers whom he never
trusted, and every hand was opened with
a gift inside, and every box we set out
had a hundred things— to tease each
mind with possibilities. I watched
Les Porter, our tireless auctioneer,
toss fifty files into a flat beer box,
cut off, then toss in fifty more, just
for good measure. Each to set there
burning on their tables of the saw horse
counters we set up out in the garage.
Never had so many people come to this
address. Cars and trucks for three blocks
every way, mad wondrous light burned in
each ear and eye as sun poured down and
Les talked on and on. He was insatiable,
a record spinning endless round and round,
and talked ten hours straight into the
dark beyond. Nothing too small or
slight for his attention. All around us
blazed up countless faces of the
living, each a candle from the wick of
her tongue speaking, or aflare in the
twin burning candles of their eyes.
Surely there would have been no wealth
of goods to give had not his fiction

saved up in the dark for forty years
the wax of all these candles for our
burning. Les talked until exhausted,
and then all fell together in the empty
room to drink champagne. Here was a life
at last spent, used up, my father nowhere
to be found, not his step on the stair,
nor pennies saving in a jar, all the budget
soda pop gone from his fridge, replaced
by wine and beer we also drank. One box
of donuts, set aside, for breakfast the
next morning— were we to live that long—
we gobbled that night in our ecstasy, or
gave to the men. Leaving all our cupboards
bare. Next morning mother came and
rescued us, uprisen from our own ashes,
coffee and toast, and golden marmalade,
the juices of the orange as out of India,
and juices of the orange as out of Florida,
and scrambled eggs like sunlight in
her frying pan.

The Arrangement

We had to do it only this way.
Somehow it came to pass, somehow
I was in the room, where
the crib in the corner sat. This is
my one strong memory of him
as a child. And it was Friday
night, or Saturday. I had this
infatuation, for Pepsi or Coke
and Wise potato chips in a
bowl, which carried still, even
at 9:30, the smell of onions and
the smell of vinegar. Why did I
not object? I didn't. Nobody did.
We were like zombies, or robots,
like the robot on TV I watched on a
Saturday morning that kept coming
on, and could not be called back,
the hero pressed against the bars.
It was the fifties, 1954 or '55.
Out in the back drive, we had
Dad's green '49 Chevy, with
the visor and the wide whitewalls
Dad scrubbed every week to make
them shine. The arrangement was
simple. We would both go to bed
at the same time, I remember the
hall light being turned off,
and then I would begin my vigil.
Lying there in the dark, my brother
in his crib, lying there, not
speaking— Did he even know how

to speak?— lying there, calming
my breathing so I might hear
over the sound of it the sound
of his. I could not go down
stairs until he was asleep— could
not watch TV with Mom and Dad
until Jeff was out for the night.
And every second waiting in the
dark I was missing something—
my heart pounded in nervousness.
My favorite shows were *Paladin*
and *Gunsmoke*. I think *Paladin*
was on first. I remember the
loud drum beat or sudden crash
of music when he presented
his card— "Wire Paladin—
San Francisco"— I think it said,
and wondered if his first name
was "Wire." Did we ever hear his
name? He had an imperious
air. A cultivated style. Among
the gangsters of the cowboy
towns, he seemed the only gentleman,
the only one who had been to school,
and could quote famous authors,
as I was learning to do, and
was kindly toward women when all
the bad guys grabbed them and
carried them off screaming. He
had a black horse, I think, and
was dressed all in black, with a
hard black hat with its cord under
his chin. Did he wear it back
on his shoulders some time?—
I cannot remember, and carried

a tiny derringer which always
saved the day. I think I got
a capgun model of it— did
we sell it at my Dad's
auction last summer?— was that
what it was?— and why it looked
familiar?— and he always won.
To draw on the bad guys, no
matter how many, and shoot them
all, while drums pounded,
announcing the finality of it all,
and how it was right, as if the
heavens themselves thundered,
then say good-bye to the
innocent and true school teacher,
and the fresh-faced kid I
knew I was like, in a town
that did not exist. He was
always leaving at the end of
the show, to get back and be
ready for the next grand foray,
the next episode, in a West
that never existed. Spouting
poetry, on a set that always
looked the same but different
too, how I never tired of his
eloquence. And sat there in
the dark with my eloquent father,
eating greasy and salty chips,
staring at the screen. We never
argued with the show, never
disagreed with the outcome.
Never wasted a bit of sympathy
on anybody shot. If you were
shot you were out, one bullet

off in your direction and you
sprawled off your horse and went
down in the dust. There was no
blood. Nobody was ever grievously
wounded or twitching. The dead
died quick and went numb,
like putting nails into boards
in my father's shop, a neatness,
a completion, without remorse,
without error. Paladin never
shot the wrong man, or overreacted,
or failed to see the extent of
the problem. Whatever needed to
be done, he was there, a great
abundance of intelligence and
justice. Upstairs, in the dark
of my brother's room, it was not
so easy. We lay there together
like two men playing dead,
trying to outsmart the other.
Hoping the upstairs clock would
move fast, and he— with nothing
in his head— he was only two
or three— would fade out quickly,
while I with my wild plan,
could lie there half the night
holding my breath. And then,
gently, as if almost in time
with my breathing, I would draw
back the covers and slip out.
I would stand by the bed, afraid
he had heard me, then tiptoe
out the door and down the hall.
Emboldened if he did not call,
I would pick up the pace,

to meet the stair tops and their
treachery. Each step on the
way down bore unseen terrors.
Each one was loose and creaked,
but you could walk on them
if you could land just right,
or if releasing a creak, stand
there a minute or two, to
represent the natural settling
of the house, night sounds we
all gloss over. Did I ever
make it down without Jeff calling?
Hearing the TV sounds, so busy
in the living room, though there
was only Mom and Dad, it seemed
a wondrous party was taking place.
Poised as I was between two
worlds, drawn on by the promise
of gunplay and music, while also
asleep in the room with my
brother, blending my breathing
with his. Trying to imagine
what I would do if he called out,
how I would make my way back, what
I would say. My usual story
was something like, I had to go
to the bathroom, and I would make
a great to-do of rattling
doorknobs, peeing and flushing
loudly, so that he might be
reassured. Then, to return to my
bed, to begin over. On nights
when I was almost down, sometimes
I'd hear the music of my shows,
and know they were on, would

stand there in exquisite pain,
feeling them slip away, their
whole vast logic and mission,
which I was now missing. And
would have to do without them
for another week. A whole long
week to be gotten through—
and was it possible?— before
I'd have another chance.
Sometimes I made it all the
way down, and would be welcomed,
like some hero for my exploits,
hogging the chips in the salad
bowl, hearing the fizz of my
Pepsi poured over the ice, and pull
my feet in slipper socks or
feet pajamas up with me
together on the couch, before
Jeff would appear in his sleeper
with feet, rubbing his eyes.
What a wonderful blend of emotions
that was— surprise, and joy
to see the sleeping son, emergent
from the dark— I see him grabbed
by my father and hugged to him,
embarrassment mixed in, to be
so caught, with me among the
adults, and would have to go
back with the tips of my fingers
greasy, back to that ruse again,
that long struggle. I don't
remember it well, cannot remember
how the process changed, how
the terms evolved. He had only
to catch me once, downstairs,

in the living room, to puncture
the myth, and so would lie there
coiled and cocked all night
like the hammer of a gun, waiting
for me to make my move. And so
it came to pass that Father
installed a lid on Jeff's crib.
How then he could not get out,
even though he knew, and so
to lie there half the night
and kick the lid with all his might.
I don't remember it, and I am
ashamed to talk of it, but it
was the fifties, and we were
without help. No Wire Paladin
or Matt Dillon came to our rescue.
Our nights were just as dark,
our problems just as tough
to solve. My father cut the board,
a big piece of paneling, which
slipped inside the crib, with leather
strips put through holes he drilled.
to tie to the slatted sides.
Maybe he even installed grommets
to keep the rawhide from breaking
through. How long it took to
bring us to this point I never
knew. Or whether I ever pretended
again. I think I did— to lie
down with Jeff in his room—
and how he would go to sleep,
and then arising to sneak out.
Did it ever matter that he
might suppose I was still there?
Or did I just gather myself up

and walk out, maybe even telling
him, "Good luck." And then the
kicking would start. He would
lie on his back and kick the lid.
His feet could just reach the
panel if he stretched. I never
saw him do it. Presumably, he
kicked and cried, until, cried out,
exhausted, he fell asleep.
Maybe Father or Mother would go
up later and remove the lid,
brush his wet hair from his face.
It was just this week I thought
of this. It came to me suddenly
driving to school. I don't know
why. Jeff died. At twenty-five.
It's fifteen years now since
his death. He lies on his back
in a cemetery a few miles from
our house. If he cries out,
no one can hear. Our father
lies beside him in the dark.

Robbing Peter to Pay Paul

I had no money, yet I had money.
I collected coins. Somehow I got
started— I think my Uncle Bill
got me going— he'd bring proof sets
every time he came, shiny coins in
envelopes, polished and bright, wrapped
up in plastic, some seal or crest
pushed in the empty slot,
the copper and the nickel and the silver—
dime, quarter, and half, all of them face
up, the Lincoln and the Jefferson, the
Roosevelt, the Washington, and then the
Franklin on the half— each one in profile,
beautifully raised and lifted out of the
obverse of the coin, detailed in their engraving,
but not too detailed so as to wear off too
soon. And you could find these coins in
change, the same faces, though not so shiny,
some with little wear, some with a lot. A
silver quarter from the early years of their
making, or one that had been kicked around,
felt different in the hand, was smooth instead
of sharp, the serrations soft instead of hard,
the eagle on the back worn down so that no
blades of the feathers could be seen— they had
a creamy feel, of things made smooth from
use, the handle of the garden hoe, from
knowing what to do, how much of the world had
they bought and sold? What had those dull eyes
seen? I would almost know, when, at the register
in Market Basket on the Boulevard, the girl

brought out a handful of quarters, that there
was one in the batch, one that had been around
the world and back again, hidden perhaps, just a
shoulder showing, its surface slightly tarnished.
The good ones— meaning the early ones— would be
worn thin, thinner than the newer stock, and I
would pick one up, holding my breath, to check
the date and mint mark. On the Washington quarter
the date was under the bust on the obverse, the
mint mark on the back beneath the crossed wreath
of the eagle. On the Jefferson nickel the date
is just to the right of LIBERTY, stamped above the
president's left ear, continuing around the curve
of the coin, the mint mark on the reverse to the
right of Monticello. The Lincoln cent carries both
date and mint mark lower right, down from the
president's nose, the dime has the mark on the
reverse next to the base of the torch, flanked
on both sides by trees or branches of trees.
The coins were beautiful, mysterious, strange
and cheap. I bought what I had for the price
of what they were— face value, trading new quarters
for old, out of the drawers at the stores, nobody
waiting on line. Those were the days you could
get Liberty Standing quarters or Barber Heads
right out of the cash registers, or I'd find
Indian Head cents and pay a penny each, no
questions asked. The girls were bored, generous
and glad to help, or watched my own obverse
complexion brighten with a find— something rare
and I'd run out of there as if my feet were lifted
on the wings of Mercury. There was a dime by
that name— Mercury Head— with tiny wings
on the face— I haven't looked at it in years,
and usually worn thin, the dates hard to read,

but all the more beautiful. I'd strain to see
what it had been, or almost make it out, and try
to turn the faded outline to its best advantage.
I was involved in kids' stuff, coins worn nearly out
and worthless— only the sharp or fine, uncirculated
coins were valuable, but one could never find them.
I lived among the old, grandfather generations,
faces so haggard, of the world's traffic— used
and abused, and almost worthless, still they'd
buy a cup of coffee, charm a child with fifty cents
to spend. I had my coin books, dark blue shiny
covers, and inside the slots to fill, each with
a date and mint mark, and the number made stamped,
millions in most cases, hundreds of millions, but
then there'd be a few with numbers in the hundred
thousands. It was the fewer the better, the
fewer meaning rarer and more valuable. And I
would learn the ones I needed, filling the rows,
always the common ones filling first, or now
and then a rare one, running down the walk
to show my Dad when he got home, might take
it out and slip it in again, or push down firm
against a hole cut small, and snap the coin
in place, never to remove again. I took them
out of circulation— some after thirty or forty
years of hard labor in the many markets of the world—
then to sleep for years in my drawers, folded
away in a coin book. Nights I might open them
before bed, and fold the pages back, and open
the books full width, all three pages, then the
liner flap, exposing the whole breadth. At first,
but a few quarters, facing left, like fish in a
school, all facing into the current, upstream,
against the flow, the Jeffersons the same,
the Lincolns turned the other way— but over

time I slowly filled the books. There were some
questionable coins, some "rare" ones I dreamed I had,
but didn't, but put my candidate into the slot,
wanting to believe. The pennies filled up fast,
especially the second book, the late forties and
fifties, then had to pencil in the new dates, 1953,
1954, the S and D, three places for all the mint
marks, no mint mark present meaning Philadelphia,
the early years being hard, the 1909 penny a
possibility, but not the S— I never saw one,
though had the special VDB, initialed for the
face designer— lodged in a secret place.
In the beginning I would take most anything,
then when I had more copies of a coin, learned
to select for wear and tear, the more new-looking
the better, and kept rotating coins in and out,
then started second backup books as better ones
turned up. They were always "turning up," a
metaphor perfectly suited to the coin, which has
two sides, a down side and an up, a head and
tails, turning if the tails were up until
the little face looked back at me, and you could
read the date, and slip it in the slot. Father
would brings coins home sometimes in his lunch pail.
Each night I'd hear him at the door, always
the same time, then rush to greet him, or he'd
get in first without me noticing, then open up
the pail wide open with the coin tucked in
the bottom next to his Thermos jug. Indian pennies
he'd bring me, or Liberty Head nickels, thick and
creamy, soft, or stained dark, with the big Roman
numeral V on the reverse, like some sort of
monument, or V for victory— which was what
it was for me to get one. I branched out into
earlier coins, the harder ones to get, started

filling up my Indian book, the Barber dime.
I kept to the smaller denominations, not having
any job, depending upon my allowance, so pennies
and nickels and dimes were usual fare, and
quarters the top of the line. I didn't save halfs—
they were too expensive. No order to the game,
just steady growth, accumulation, a collection
always in flux. There was always something
going on, Father would find a strange nickel in
change, or Mother had a quarter— did I want it?—
then would I take it and go run up to my desk
and get my coin books out, my magnifying glass,
my book of values, and look it up. Or Uncle Bill
might come with proofs, and add to my collection.
I could be amazed. Paul was collecting too, but
mostly stamps. And had huge albums filled with
gorgeous colors, the papers strangely frail— while
I preferred the weight of coins, the value in hand,
the way I'd rub my fingers over them and thoughts
would come, or worries melt away. Then Paul
started collecting coins as well. His father, rich,
with nothing else to do, no other children. Paul
had me down one time to view some new things
that he'd got. He laid them out on a piece of
velvet, for proper viewing. There in the midst
of many coins I knew was one incredible piece,
a tiny flake of silver, the famous three-cent piece,
made in the eighteen hundreds, thin as paper, soft
and bendable, delicately cut, with images upon it
that looked like ghosts, or the soft imprint of
a moth's wings. I couldn't take my eyes off it,
could not look at Paul for the envy he would see
in me, then stole it when he wasn't looking.
I remember my fierce walk back the block to home,
the slender coin down in my pocket, then put

my little hand in there to grasp it— wanting to
run, wanting never to stop, wanting to take it out
and look at it, then did, upstairs in my room,
and set it on the blotter under the desk lamp—
so beautiful. I kept it maybe an hour, then
confessed, and took it back, the long walk back
to Paul's, Paul and his father leaning out their door,
and told my story how the coin had fallen in my cuff,
unknown to me until I got back home. Handing it
back, like all the world's gold, or answer to
every prayer. And the shame of it. They
would not come out on the porch, but stood there
with their door just ajar, so as not to let me
near them. How they must have known I took it,
but let me spare myself. Paul soon outstripped me
in the coin department. I had no money to keep up.
He would go to the hobby store in Utica, each
week or so, come back with little envelopes with
treasures. He bought the whole range of copper-nickel
Indian Head cents, the early ones, thick as nickels,
with a delicate brassy complexion, beautifully
inscribed feathers, their words and numbers
sharply raised. Each one could cost ten dollars at
least. I went there once with Dad, and stared down
through the glass cases as the coins came up, row
on row on circulating sets of shelves, beautiful things,
and gold too, the same gorgeous faces but in gold!
The world was rich. And I was not. Rich and various—
would I ever exhaust its endless beauty? Joe Giltnan
lived next door. Turned out he was a coin collector
too, and one day had me over. What I took I can't
remember, maybe my quarter book. We sat on his bed
and he got out his coins, stack on stack of Liberty
Standing halfs, everything I liked in quarters but on
a larger scale. I think I wanted to rob them too.

And came away defeated. And yet strangely charged,
as if electrified. It was Joe who had the old car
in his drive, a '48 or '49 Chevy, two-toned green,
and drove it back and forth, like grinding something
up, the way Art Nebelsik did next door to us in
Crete, thirty years later, grinding the husks off
black walnuts from the recent fall. Joe was
practicing, putting the car in gear, going forward
ten or twelve feet, shifting to another gear, then
screeching to a stop. Less than a year later
he was dead, killed on Thanksgiving Day, crossing
a fence out hunting— a buddy shot him in the head.
Three young men died on our block alone, Joe
that Thursday, then a few years later Ricky Adams—
in a car like Jeff, then Jeff— it was a sad street.
You go past the houses now and you can feel it—
something gone out of them there, or maybe just
the trees cut down. Stark now, bright and naked,
emptier. I don't know how long I collected coins.
Stealing from Paul had maybe changed things, or
Joe's death. The world intruded. Though
I have known collectors who never stop— Chester
Williams stuck to his guns right to the end. Why
do we collect things? Is it because we will die?
Some small act of saving something from the teeth
of time. I used to like to find a coin that was
really chewed up, something dented from a bullet
maybe, or a BB, pounded on, or the pennies Dad
gave me which he said he had put on the rails,
and watched the train roll over them, completely
squished on one side, half the penny ballooning out,
flat smooth. Or the beautiful dime Father had
carved with his initials on the back, the face
the same as you'd expect, but letters like a sailboat's
sails floating on a tiny sea on the reverse. How

did he guide me through these years? What famous
saying to learn from, or learn the wisdom of too
late through tears? Robbing Peter to pay Paul?
No, it was the other way— robbing Paul to pay
myself, which did not work. Or maybe he foresaw
what happened later, how I'd come to need the money.
There were things to buy, a girl to take out, a
record I had to have. For years I'd had my horde,
no pressing reason to go there, not even to look—
slightly ashamed for hiding coins away when other
boys were pounding baseballs down at Franklin's
Field. My secret life. Then it ended. One day
I needed a buck or two, and there was my quarter
book— nearly complete. I had so many, and so
took the common ones, knowing I could find them
easily again, when times got good. I never put
them back. Each week another thing I needed,
taking the common ones, closing the book, closing
the drawer, forgetting it. Robbing from myself
to pay myself. Robbing from the
boy who saved them, each and every precious one,
instead of buying a Popsicle or gum, clutching
his precious quarter, squirreling it away, out
of the world's light. Robbing my childhood of
itself, to save the money I should have spent in
fun, some innocence that did not matter anymore.
How in the sixth grade it had ended, the day I
took my coin collection in, and tried to show them
what it meant, but could not find the words.
Nobody cared. And let Paul take the silver
dollars out, my pride and joy, and stacking them
in hand, go around the room trying to draw recruits.
I can't believe I let Paul do that, letting the
coins click together, scratching them, even the
uncirculated ones which Father won from that

special roll, all the same date and mint mark,
like brand new. My very best and still not good
enough. Like Crusoe, I'd go to my room, high in
the house, to pillage what remained, the wreck
that once had been his life. Everything had
changed. The boys so tall, the girls grown
beautiful. And Paul gave up collecting and took
up tennis, collected tennis balls instead—
he had a whole huge gym bag full, which he used
to practice his serve and overheads— the shot
I couldn't hit— his father hitting them
to him, over and over, until Paul could not
miss. I wanted those tennis balls, instead
of my three gray flat ones and my flimsy
racket. I followed after Paul, looking to
trade my coins in for another life, but never
found that new thing I was supposed to want.
The quarter books are nearly empty now. My
last withdrawal I bought a gift for Mom,
not even lying to myself that I would put
them back. I spent my childhood as we all
do. My comics Jeff got later, sold to buy
drugs, and my best 45s, Elvis and the Beatles,
all the famous stuff. I never knew a Peter,
but for the guy I later taught tennis to.
He was a little fat kid in Crete, 1300 miles
from Rome, where we live now, who had a crush
on Barb. We used to go up to the field house
at Doane, on weekends, letting ourselves in
with the keys we rented, set up the nets
and play all night. I beat him maybe a
thousand times, still have these vivid images
of him coming in to net, then I lobbing over
his head, wearing him out, thinning him down.
He never forgot, and calls us to this very

All That Is Not Given Is Lost

day. Ten years after, his own childhood over,
he talked me into entering a tournament,
"Class-B doubles," which we won. Before the
match I took him in to buy some carbonated
juice, and health food bars, and energy pills
for me at 50. Spent, I think, 20 or 30 bucks.
Took all the old quarters out of my books,
and dropped them on the counter, turned them
all into tennis shots and serves. I never
played so well. We splurged in every way,
were generous with each other, setting each
other up on the court. I think I hit a
dozen overheads, the sort of shot I always
failed at. Paul Ruby and I paired at doubles
for the tennis team, how they always hit to me,
the weaker one, the overhead my weakest shot.
These two young Lincoln guys must have read
the old scouting reports, so lobbed me half
the afternoon, then watched in disbelief
as I put every one away, hitting to the open
court, the way coach tried to teach me thirty
years before, laughing the whole time, patting
Peter on the back. He's a big guy now, strong
as they come, who carried me for most of two
sets, forgiving me my coin collector's squint,
until my pills kicked in, and then I carried
him. We won first place in our division—
it took me thirty years to win a championship
at last. Peter and Paul? To spark across
that gap of time— robbing from Paul in
1953, paying Peter, 1994, forty years the spark
stored up across that endless interval,
lighting up our faces in our joy.

Warren

Warren Fine was a great writer.
I read a novel of his once,
and it was the real thing.
An unpublished book— from
the years of his "decline." I read
another book of his after his death,
forty pages of *In The Animal Kingdom.*
There were no two sentences alike,
and not a single one I'd ever seen.
That's the sort of writer he was.
Daring and original and strange.
I stopped reading the book. It was
too much work. Besides, I said,
Warren's dead. What does it matter?
If I did not think to read him
while he lived, what does it
matter now. That's a problem
I have— appreciating people after
they're dead. Then you think
of all the things you should have done.
I should have had him out to the
house more. We could have
carried him around from room
to room. My kids never forgot
the time Warren went out
walking with us after midnight.
He kept falling down on people's
lawns. By then he'd nearly
finished off the fifth.
Earlier he pitched to Jackie
with the whiffle ball,

recounting his baseball exploits.
Warren was a good drunk.
Or then he was. What did he
live after that?— ten more years?
How young we were. If only
I could have given him...
If only I could have loved
him more. And so on. If
the dog, my father said, hadn't
stopped to pee, he'd still be
running. A legion of "ifs."
I walked around like that for
weeks. I felt responsible.
Sunlight indicted me. The
wind. A look at his pitiful
car he'd bought with an NEA,
which he summarily wrecked,
a fender at a time, a busted
tail light, stains on the seats,
rust, a twisted bolt, tires
going flat. The very image of the
man himself. His fingers
would be all stained from
cigarettes. I've never seen
hands like that. The whole
hand yellow from nicotine.
Did he never wash? Did he
smoke that much? Whose
voice was gravel over rocks.
And came from far away,
as if it had to collect
itself, as if perhaps it had
forgotten itself. Then came
on strong and sure, like a
mountain stream, cold to

the touch. Mornings I would
see him in the mail room.
You could smell the booze.
He'd be disagreeable, the
sort of disagreeable you love
when someone's got a reputation
for it and does it, just to
oblige, to mark the morning with.
How I'd see Warren in the hall,
and sure enough, it was the
man himself, no change,
no improvements, just the steady
weather of his griefs. He'd
mutter something about money,
or bills, a constant worry,
then teeter off to teach
his morning class. Mornings
were for writing, though he
couldn't write. But hated
the chair for sticking him in
morning classes when
he should have been home
writing. He was matter-of-
fact about it. How can I
write? he'd say, and meant
it. Warren never game up
believing he was a writer.
If all that he could do was
write a line, he was a writer
still. He never lost his
dignity, never cried out
forlorn against his fate.
After it became clear he
couldn't do novels anymore,
could not concentrate to do

novels, or sit there in a
chair that long and type,
he took up poetry.
His prose was fierce and
unforgiving, but his poems
were just the opposite, soft,
sentimental, full of little
indulgences. He wrote
about love, about lovers,
about joy in the arms of love,
and you would wonder to
yourself how anyone could
stand his breath, or his
cold hand. Women loved
him, to their credit,
and he wrote them love songs.
Warren never gave up on
love either. Right to
the end he gloried in it.
It was a man's right,
a person's birthright.
He was never shy about
the need, or the machinery.
Still, it marked a retreat.
Who could write hundreds
of pages of bristling prose
like wind out of the north,
and then to end his life
in love songs, songs
like the radio. His plan,
that last fatal summer,
was to take up teaching
poetry that fall. We
were supposed to meet,
and talk about the course.

Another way I let him
down. The day he died
Fred was out to fire him
for not showing up
for the first day of classes.
Warren was home, dead,
the telephone cord wrapped
around his body. He had
been trying to call for help,
to anyone in his final terror.
Mike found the body.
I think he'd be lying there
still for all the people
who cared. The funeral
was a bleak affair, but
afterwards we met his
family. It was all
strange, as strange as any
page of his prose. No one
had understood him. No
one had known the breadth
of his genius. We were
left with the dirt, the
sandwiches on white bread,
the long drive back in the cars.
Only a handful of Lincoln
people went. When you
saw that, you knew you
would never want that
to happen ever again.
A corner of a graveyard
in Kansas. What was it
all about? Some pain he
never got over? Early
success, and then having

to live beyond it, to live
dying to have it back again.
Or just the booze.
Leaning on it, writing
with it, writing in spite
of it, and then not
writing at all, alone
in the room with the booze.
After Warren died I stopped
drinking. He had had
enough for both of us.
Drifted around, felt
sorry for myself, wrote
some lame half-hearted
elegies. I had followed
him right to the edge of
the grave, and then I
stood there, teetering
on the edge. I could
go in too, and give it
up, but something stopped
me. It was nothing he
said. No words to
inscribe on the wall.
Maybe a bird singing
or the sun come down
to lie along the ground
on Warren's grave.
Maybe it was the ride
back with Pat and Sally,
listening to them talk,
saying I would build on
this, I would start here.
We drove on over the
hills as the sun set,

heading home. The
world was still there.
For all the pain, for
all the misery of trying
and failing and not
finding, for all the
betrayals, for all the
anger you felt, it was
still there. Warren
left his green baseball
cap to anyone who wanted
it. I took it and his
lighter, but I put the
hat away, and gave the
lighter to my daughter.
One day I stopped thinking
about him. Today, in the
office, I made a joke
about his drinking,
compared it to my need
for candy. Then I
knew I'd made the journey.

And If I Had a Lever Long Enough I Would Move the Earth

He did not have this lever, was consigned
to small pliers and wrenches, had a crowbar
that he'd sharpen now and then, to put a good
edge to it, for prying boards apart, would rap
his knuckles on the end around, where the wrench
slipped off the frozen nut, under the hood of the
car, and cry out, the knuckles bleeding, the nut
that would not turn, no matter how he pulled on
it. The earth lay beyond, flat on its endless back,
gone off in all directions of birds and trees, the
roads gone endless into other roads, and smaller
roads, then onto the very grit of the land, and
throw the dust up in our mirror— we could go
like that, of a Saturday, to see how big the
world was, and off the beaten track, then where
the road ended in a circle of confusion, strike
out boldly on some footpath into the trees,
get lost, or circle back, or break on through, to
find the river flowing cheerily over the rocks,
headed somewheres else. We never got to the
end, nor fell off the edge, no matter how far
out he got, at the end of the arm of some road,
or pry bar, lifting up a big flat of slate, down
by Fish Creek, to build our patio. Or drive into
the night, into the very teeth of night, the very
throat, the world dimmed out to faint lights
in store windows, the traffic lights on simmer,
blinking softly as the snow fell, would end
at Nani's house, some new beginning. Come

summer, we would head north with the tent,
load the old truck-body trailer, which he'd built,
with the old spoked wheels, the tires such an odd
and inconvenient size, he worried always about flats,
but never had one, all those years, but babied them
going north, at a snail's pace— loaded down under the
weight of all the things we barely lifted on, the giant
canned goods cabinet, with the angle-iron legs, each
one sharpened to a shiny point, so that with the
legs screwed in place, would sink into the sand,
sink of its own vast weight, like the *Titanic*.
The stove an odd contraption too, cast iron, covered
with lovely cast-iron flowers, the burners massive,
with the legs and platform tucked under, the whole
thing fastened with heavy bolts. At camp we would
assemble it, and place the propane tank beneath,
where there each morning Mother would fry eggs.
Not like these modern back-pack stoves that weigh
but ounces, it weighed as much as a canoe,
and all that you could do would be to carry it
into some remote pond, then stand there in a swarm
of Adirondack flies and fry your eggs, yolks
of the loon, stolen in the moonlight. A critic of
our pop culture and the age of the disposable—
life?— wife?— washing machine or book— he hated
flimsy paperbacks whose spines snapped if you tugged
on them too hard— hated how things were not
made to last, remembering the iron age and the
Age of Bronze, vast monumental structures, doors
two stories tall, against which a man was
dwarfed, could hardly reach the knob,
and the great machines of another age, like I
saw once at a mill, powered by water, the huge
flywheel, the great shafts big around as my waist—
or photos of the giant three-bladed, brass ship

propeller, stranded on a truck beside the road,
two stories high or higher— that is the sort of
company he kept, if not in person, then in the
romance of books. The tent, for camping in the
summer, which nowadays would be some gossamer film
like the fog upon my glasses coming into the
warm kitchen from out of the cold back porch,
or roll up like an umbrella, and fit neatly under
one arm, or snug in a pouch of the pack, was
instead a great monstrosity of folds, fold
after fold, and the great high peak, which must
have been twelve feet high, pitched on the long
wooden poles, big around as my arm, and which he'd
built a special rack for off the side of the
trailer, and had to hang a flag on, waving red
the whole 80 miles. The tent a light tan color,
"light- weight," they called it, though you could not
lift it, and even folded tight, with the screened-
in porch rolled separate, and put in its special
bag, it made a package big as a desk. The floor
was a dark brown color, and treated with water-
resistant chemical, "impregnated," I think he
called it, and very heavy. The stakes were various,
but the more prominent of all were the long oak
ones, actually two sizes, the long ones and the
longer ones, the longer ones being over two feet
in length, maybe two and a half, and thick, notched
in two places. These were used for ropes from the
peaks, guide ropes out from the high peak, a
couple stakes strategically placed, to keep the
skin of the tent taut, and then across the front,
two guides for every pole. It would take hours
to set the tent, after the ground was raked, after
the ground was swept, to rid the surface of stones
that might poke through the fabric, or bruise a toe

come midnight staggering out to pee in the moonlight.
Then a black thick plastic sheet would go down,
to keep the floor from getting damp. Along
the back of the tent, he had designed a wonderful
feature, where the whole wall would roll up, and
could be tied, every few feet, to ties that hung
down from the wall, thus opening the back to breezes
and the gaze of passersby. Otherwise zipped down
tight for the night, against the dark, against
marauding bears that might come through, making a
solid wall. It was big as a house— some people
even said that where they came from, their house
was not much larger, two rooms, one for sleeping and
dressing, the other the kitchen, and for looking out
upon the rain that dripped all day from hemlocks.
At the peak of the summer season in the fifties,
we could have 8 or 10 people huddled together
under the sagging front awning, some playing cards
at the heavy steel "portable" table, it took me
years to grow up strong enough to carry. Father
would every now and then take a dish towel he had
draped around his neck, and ball it up around his
fist, then push it up against some big belly of
rain that sagged the roof down between angled
support poles, some "flaw in the design," he
puzzled, and which sagged even after he added the
auxiliary poles, to crisscross the large rectangle
of canvas, the way, on campus, kids will cut the
corners on their way to class, necessitating
more and more sidewalks, each bisecting the angle,
until the whole grass field is paved. We
would cook on iron, huge cast-iron pans,
darkened with grease and heat, the bottoms caked
it seemed with hard fat or tar, which came off
on your hands, pans that were never dried with a

towel, but with paper towels instead, and the
dark come off, pans soaked in grease, tempered
by hot fat, "impregnated" he might say, thus
heavier, more weighty than before. Each fish
we fried, the pans became more ponderous, took on
the smell of fish oil, or the smell of onions,
so that the next thing we cooked smelled with the
ghost of fish, our breakfast pancakes fragrant with
trout smell and the choke of peppers. Setting the
tent, late in the day, if the traffic had been bad,
the long lines at the gate, he might seem to regret
the length of the stakes he had to pound into
the unforgiving ground. But would go at it
indefatigably, lifting the huge one-bladed ax,
bringing the heavy flat side down, precisely,
moving the stake an inch or two, and might get
one in part way, only to have it hit a rock and
start to twist, or sometimes break one off entirely,
then start over, cursing lightly. Maybe twenty blows
and one was properly seated, angled off ten feet
or so from the uprising wall of the tent, me holding
the corner pole, Jeff on the other rope. It would
go up at the corners, first one sagging upwards
or the rest of it sagging down, misshapen, like
a disaster in the middle of itself, happening around
us, Dad crawling under the flattened canvas,
threading the poles in, reaching back to have me
hand him the big heavy ridge, made of steel pipe,
screwed together in the middle with a big fitting,
big fittings on the ends for the pole pins to slip
through. Into the dark of the flat space we were
going to live in for two weeks, threading the poles
under the canvas, I can still hear the scrape the
poles made against the hard dry canvas, like a
zipper almost. Then rising, up on one knee perhaps,

the comedy of the man under the canvas, making
all sorts of shapes, like the misshapen figures in
clouds— what was he now?— a horse without
a head?— a bookcase under a blanket?— some mythic
figure trying to free itself, marbles of Michelangelo—
trying to break free from their stone— to struggle
there in the dark, trying to get it right, wearing
the whole tent's weight fully upon his back and shoulders
of everything he planned and built, while in the
clearing in the fading light we laughed and joked.
He was tenacious, clinging like a sloth to its branch,
hugging the heavy tent around him, of the cloth
he'd chosen, the weight he wanted, to keep back
the world, or marching with the 12-foot ridge,
like Lancelot unhorsed, still valiant against some
daunting foe off there beyond the shadows in the
growing dusk. The tent he'd designed himself, ordered
from Milvo Awning and Tent Works, beautifully sewn,
to last forever if the rats wouldn't get it, or the
mildew— coming back each summer from our two weeks
in the rain at Raquette Lake, would have to hang
the whole thing in the attic of the house, to stagger
up the stairs with it, dripping wet, three times its
former weight, then up the fragile attic stairs,
into the spacious room of the attic. I helped
him do it many times, ropes knotted, then threaded
through the grommets where the ridge poles went,
then the peaks hoisted up, and wrapped around a
special pin he'd lodged in the roof beam, then to
lift the other side as well, stretching the tent
room out beneath, one house inside another as it were.
He was tireless. We'd taken down the camp in pouring
rain, again, getting out by noon, on the assigned
day to leave, loading all the sopping stuff into
the trailer, then the two long hours down the

twisty road back home again, then to unload.
Before nightfall we'd have the tent hung up to dry
in the attic, or filling the whole double garage,
a house within a house, surreal and lovely in the
inside of the place we stored our cars, safe
at last out of the rain. He knew how to do things,
knew about mechanical advantage, knew about pulleys
and screws, was always twisting some jack wheel
with the long rod of the handle, lifting the heavy
car up for its oil change. He did his own work, was
loath to ask for help, was loath to pay another
man for that which he might do himself, or teach to
me. I never learned except one lesson broadly
emblazoned on everything he did— to let others do
these things that steal our lives away, that were
his life's full measure and devotion— to save me
for another day, which is today. The oil I never
changed has saved me for this poem, the brakes I
never fixed, the stakes I never drove, hard into
unyielding rock, of that broad granite shelf with
its thin skin of soil, upon which Father had
determined to set up our camp I saved for dreaming,
watching the clouds go by, lying on my back under
the shade of hemlocks on the one day maybe that it
did not rain up country. Being so locked down
onto the ground, hammered home, bolted,
staked down and pulled taut by guide ropes,
with a big toolbox in the trunk, weighing the
car down, too heavy for me to lift, which he
would have to lift and lug, filled with all
manner of wrenches and pliers and saws and hammers,
he must have dreamed, like me, but not of clouds,
but of some ultimate advantage, some tool whose
handle was so very long he might stand out of
sight of the world's work, not having the dirt of

it under his nails, of the rock he was trying to
lift, or the grease from the bolt he was trying to
free from being even more locked down than he—
to stand on some remote ledge, enjoying the view,
of both the earth and heaven, while gentle breezes
blew in the back of the tent to cool him as he
lifted gently. Far from the heave of the earth's
storm and strife, and the damp cold mildew of the
ground, to plague him all his waking days and sleepless
nights, exhausted from his labors, endless upon earth
and time— far from the sweat that beaded up his
forehead underneath the problem of the weight he'd
forced upon himself, for strength, and how it had
to last— now, with a lever long enough, he only had
to lift one finger, just a tiny lift, the way you'd
beckon, across the room discreetly in some fancy
restaurant where he'd never gone, to signal for
the check perhaps, or to complain, discreetly,
that the white wine was too chill. And have it all
figured out at last, the fulcrum placed, somewhere
beyond Brazil, the lever tip wedged perhaps
under Brazil's big hump, the mad Atlantic swirling
all around, the sharks circling, curious, as to the
vast point of good wood— oak like the tent stakes,
but of no earthly tree, the grain long and straight,
ten thousand miles at least, brought from some other
galaxy— and there at the end, where his one hand
might grasp it if he cared to, special-made for him—
a delicate handle carved, with maybe just an indentation
for his pinky finger, just the tip, where it might
be inserted. So, that, if he cared to, some afternoon,
nothing else to do, no chores left to eat the day
away to nothing in the twilight come, the twilight
of his years too soon to come, and still more work,
unfinished, never to be done— and leave no time for

All That Is Not Given Is Lost
97

play— instead perhaps he might come back, from fishing
in the Pleiades, or on some other aimless walk beyond
the stars, might lift that pinky finger and the
earth would move.

The Spider on the Windowsill

Barb painted the sill last week
and its foot stuck to the strip
along the edge. Or I did it.
Or I like to think it was out
walking and Barb drew her brush
along the edge and a few bristles
ran over an outstretched foot
of the spider. Brushing by the
way the traffic does, and we are
almost under the wheels, the wind
blowing back our hair at the crosswalk.
We found it a week later. It was
still there, in the same spot, on the
sill of the north window in our
daughter's room. Saturday to Saturday,
while we were living our lives, going
to school, fretting and worrying.
I played racquetball four times, twice
with Rick, twice with Paul,
ecstatic to get on the court after
the long frustrating days in class.
Got some manuscripts back, sulked
in my office, dabbled a little on the
computer, wrote a few letters, sent
the books out again. I had wanted
to give up, and throw in the towel.
One book's been rejected seven
times in the past six months. I
had made multiple copies— which made
my heart skip a beat— on the unlikely
chance the book would be

taken twice on the same day,
and I would have to choose, and
make another enemy. Meanwhile
the spider waited. There might have
been a moment right away that with
some awesome effort it might have
yanked its stuck foot free. But the
paint was the quick-dry variety,
and locked up fast. And there was
the strong smell of it too, which
must have made its eyes tear.
We didn't go back to the room.
Barb was busy in school, ten classes
a day, sudden shifts from science
to German to theatre to art,
her inventions unit, which involved
the whole school, her ambassadors
of her own making, which meets
before school on Fridays,
and in the evenings our frantic
meals, before I'm off to the
library for a night of study.
There were all kinds of crises.
We had a visiting poet, who
was coming to one of my classes,
which I fretted over. Monday
I worked hard late reading over
her new book, trying to do a
preview reading in my classes,
trying to do justice to her
without envy or rancor— remembering
my conduct of six years back,
where I would welcome them
and then betray them in a
review. Which I can hardly

talk about, it seems so awful
now. Remembering that, trying
to make up for it, trying to be
attentive and respectful, trying
to become Karen Swenson, and
think like she does. There I
was sitting in my chair in a
study carrel at Doane Library,
reading the book over and over,
trying to absorb Karen Swenson
into my very being. Meanwhile
the spider settled down. It sat,
or perhaps rather, lay, flat on
the windowsill, dropping the weight
of its body down firmly onto the sill
(which we did not hear, being
busy in the kitchen), taking the
weight off its legs. It shifted
to get comfortable, or rubbed the
trapped leg with one of its
other legs, to keep the circulation
up, to prevent cramping.
Later there were noises in the house.
Squirrels chased each other
across high sections of the roof,
and once, maybe it was around
midweek, midday on a Wednesday
perhaps, a squirrel came
down the side of the house,
and, clinging to the stucco siding
with its nails, and latching
onto a few old vines with its feet,
hung there beside the window
and looked in. Perhaps the
spider saw him, or perhaps it

was sleeping then. Karen arrived,
we did the class. I was pretty
nervous. I saw right away she
was not going to talk about the
book I read, and tried to steer her
to it, on account of all the
questions I had made. We
struggled for a few minutes,
maybe ten, I trying to
attach myself more firmly to
her, she trying to break free.
We were like a spider stuck on
a glass plate, like a spider
and its mirror image. Everything
she did I countered her. Everything
I did she countered me. Until,
exhausted, we surrendered.
The students sat there the whole
time, as if they were themselves
the ones trapped, and did not
interfere, did not come to our
rescue. And then the remorse,
like waves over me, clamped
down in my chair in my office,
afraid to be seen, ashamed of
myself for having imposed myself,
and for our weird dancing in
public. Somehow, by an effort
almost superhuman, I dragged myself
out of my chair and climbed
the stairs, and went in to where
Karen was talking, and apologized.
Had I not would I be
sitting there still? And the
world gone by me in a rush?

Kuzma

Stuck in the tar of remorse,
and almost lost. Meanwhile the
spider was spending a long week.
Mostly it slept, mostly it just
lay there. Outside the window
the world's weather paraded
itself. And then the end of
the parade, a few stragglers,
the remnants of a band, a little
movement in the branches of the
cedar tree, a swish of green
across the window pane. Of
course it got very hungry. Barb
and I were out to dinner at an
expensive restaurant. A tiny
chip of spiced lamb fell off
my fork to the table top. The
spider could have kept alive
a year on what I could not see.
Then it was Friday night.
Another party at the country
club. A night of golf, then
dinner at a steak house. I got
involved in a long political
discussion with Steve Rische.
I was astonished he knew so
much, astonished that I could
follow what he said. We sat there
for two hours, locked in our
chairs, as the chaos of the
evening passed around us. I did
not hear another voice, or even
eat my food. It was like
young love, entirely transfixed.
The next day at last was

Saturday. It's the day Barb
and I have reserved for
working on the house. I slept
in as usual, she up at nine.
But by eleven-thirty we were
gathering the tools. I was
to be outside primarily, scraping
brown paint off the window,
where I had been in a hurry
six or seven years before—
who was this maniac of six
or seven years before? How
did we live? Up on the ladder
on the north side I found a
comfortable position, while
Barb looked over our paint job
from the week before and worked
sewing the curtains she was
putting up. We talked to each
other through the window. It
was a mild day. "What's this?"
Barb said. A spider stuck
to the paint. With the tip
end of her fingernail she
cut the tiny tip of the spider's
leg off, setting it free.
On one of my trips inside to
get coffee and look at my
work from the other side, I
saw the spider. One of its
eight legs was noticeably
shorter. There it was,
running back and forth
along the window ledge. An
hour later I was back inside

for more coffee, admiring
the work. The spider was
still there. It seemed
very excited.

Bill

Bill called me, the only time in forty years
he's called me. I should have known something
was up, but I was so startled, and everything
went so fast, it was over before I knew.
But all very matter-of-fact. Not brace
yourself, not sit down and then I'll tell you
what you must already know. Things happen
for Bill. Nothing happens, nothing happens,
nothing happens, and Bill just goes along day
after day, the sunlight on the table, the
calendar turning, the blue light of the TV,
and Bill does not remark the shape of
time, and Bill does not stay up all night,
his face pressed to the window of the future
staring in trying to see. Then another day
of nothing happens. Then something happens.
My father has a heart attack. In the
hospital. Then I get a phone call from
Bill. "Your father's had a heart attack,"
he says. "He's not going to make it."
That's how the word goes forth, into
the world. No flourishes, no eloquence
except the facts. Letting the facts
speak. I am not immune. I am of
this stock. I deepen the corners of
rooms with worry, I shadow the corners
of facts with fears, and all my famous
rehearsed regrets that play a hundred
nights, to get the lines right, but I
know, I think I am learning, the
weight of facts. My father, yes, I

know the man, your father, yes,
and I will not be there to hold his hand,
or lean to whisper love in his ear,
has had a heart attack. No
quiver in his voice. Emotionless.
Not even excitement of having a
story to share, who never had a
story to share, a story anybody'd
care to hear. Who could be in a room
where many talked, and some would nearly
leap from their skins, to turn themselves
inside out, while Bill would sit there
the whole time, not even his forehead
creased. Some boulder shouldering above
the onslaught of the stream, with all
the water in its wild array around him,
running on and on, and in the middle
of the torrent, Bill sits quietly, his
hands in his lap. Eyewitness to
history, I would like to say, waiting
for all the mad press of people in
their turmoil to expire, worn out
in their fury, to tell the telling
fact or two. Your father's in the
hospital, Bill says, the house around
him empty, the connection good.
Waiting with his message forty
years. All the rest preliminaries,
subterfuge or illusion. The time
of someone's graduation, silence, or the
day of the big storm, silence, or when
my mother moved from out of the
house, her necessary furniture, silence,
or when my brother died and there was
such a mad scramble of people trying

to rewrite time, trying to pump heat
and light back into dead limbs, or look
for the spark of life still blooming
in a face, a face with a life, where
life had gone out of a face, what
poetry did Bill provide? Silence.
Who was known by the silences he
kept. Who in the midst of anger or
inflation or depression's dark flurry
of dark silks would not be moved.
Who had looked on the grief of the
ages, and, seeing nothing special to
remark, folded his hands. So when
I heard his voice on the phone,
clear and crisp and strong, but
distant too, I knew something was
up, some other chapter we had not
yet read, over in back in the
far reaches of some book Bill had
never opened or read in yet.
Your father, I think was his phrase,
and so on, spoken this one time
here, on the phone, his poetry.
It is easy to find fault. To ask
of the world to be what we ask
of the world. To listen in yourself
for what you need, and, turning
to that person from whom nothing
has come, like a dead planet, strung
out in some distant orbit, far
from the sun, or like I will do in
class, after months of silence from
a quarter of the room, to scan
my eyes along the faces there,
feeling for words, for life.

And what do you think? I
want to say, but won't, being of
that stock, that icy bend of a
limb to the family tree on
which no bird has come to
sing, but a dead leaf maybe
blows, declaring how once the
world was good, the world was
summer. Bill's got his detractors.
And many others who, upon meeting
him, cannot remember. He offers
nothing, my mother likes to say.
Someone who— when he dies— she
likes to go on, kicking a dead horse
in the mouth, the world will not
notice, will not be better or worse,
will not even pause. Who dies,
and a car door slamming packs more
urgency, and we wait for the motor
to start, and we wait to be driven up
and away. But I do not wish for what
I do not have, being grateful and in
love with what I have. Bill's a
great uncle, mother says, who never
gave a gift or winked across a room
or told a joke, or kidded you, or
told you to get out of there, have a
good time, or anything. I see
him as a mask, a sphinx. He is
for me a mask of life, where,
though unchanging, over its face
play the great arousals and
conflagrations, a screen to put the
movie on, or maybe like the Mona
Lisa, an inscrutable look, with, if

you look at it long enough, there
in a dim floodlight behind the skin
is the warm glow of the world. Some
minimal heat, some animal
strength. There is no probing his
mystery. Exasperated you come
away, and want to pull your last
few hairs out. Sue says "Bill,"
and, adding him up in his entirety,
you can see it, seeing the lights
flashing in her eyes like apples
and plums in a slot machine, in
two or three seconds, having it all
come up, rung up, and not being
again, a winning combination,
but a dud, smiles, shrugs.
Mark, my son, from watching
Bill ignore me, turn away, walk
from the room, turn chilly at my
jokes, not speak to me for hours
in a room, wouldn't give him the
Colorado Buffaloes baseball cap
Bill wanted, when, in an incredible
assertion of self and purpose, Bill
requested it. I tried to tell
Mark, it doesn't matter what Bill
says, it doesn't matter what Bill
won't or will do, I like him,
I understand, I don't want him
to change. Something he took from
life, some knee he learned it on,
some necessary angle on the whole
wild stupid issue. So, he is not
emotional. Then, in his presence,
where there is in evidence some

small measure of emotion, then we
can grin and exchange glances, the
highfliers among us, the tall-masted
schooners of the heart, who register
any small breeze, and hurry off
somewhere on their self-important
ways, we can go skimming over
the bay to celebrate this glory
day, the day that Bill said thanks,
or smiled. But the sphinx is
not inscrutable. Undergoing dialysis
makes the sphinx wear, and cannot
even keep its mask on straight—
so when asked in a cheery mood
how the day went— says "Lousy."
When asked what the sphinx wants
for supper, the answer comes
as from the oracle— "Nothing,
I'm not hungry." And so you
build another cockeyed level to
the myth, who, uneating night
after night, sits in the morning
in the kitchen, waiting for his ride
to come. For whom a whole day
of attentive nurses and whirring
machines, chrome and electric,
what kept some genius up and
spoiled his sleep for years,
reduced to "Lousy." Or no appetite.
If in the waking world Bill
keeps himself in reserve, saving
his strength for now and then,
every forty years or so, some
essential message— the right
messenger for the wrong message—

in sleep he is not so
locked inside himself. One
night after my father died, and we
were all together in the house,
looking at my father's guns
and making dreams together out of
his many privacies, Bill, from
sleep in his adjoining room,
cried out my father's name not once,
not twice, but over and over,
and each time, I think, melted the
snow a little that lay on the
roof of the house of our regard.
We have these people in the world.
They are incomplete, not what we'd
wish for on a trip across Europe, for
instance, who could stare at a whole
landscape and never blink, for
whom everything in consciousness
is given, or too strange— which
is it?— to acknowledge. From
sleep, however, the brother speaks.
Brother to brother, hearing or
thinking that he heard, my father's
step upon the stairs, or the
creak of a board in the hall,
where maybe my daughter ran
down the hall and stairs for more
coffee. "Harry," he called.
For half an hour pretty much
answering my father's inquisitions.
Reassuring him. Letting him
know he was OK. To the point
where you wanted to say, yes,
we have gone far enough into

this strange country where these
men set up household and loved
each other in the world. And
then another night, a similar
scene, with Barb and I alone,
sorting papers, fondling objects,
looking for traces of a life,
Bill cried out again in sleep,
not this time to answer and to
reassure, but to inquire after Harry's
health. Which maybe marked a recent
memory, of just before my father
died, in his final illness, which
he diagnosed as flu, and fed with
cough drops and Robitussin, which
we found beside his bed, a nub
of a cough drop, one of those
chewy ones, which he had given
up on, and removed from his mouth,
and which I liked to see setting
there. I am not immune to these
revelations of character or imagination
or affection. These men are mine.
I bear them in the carriage of
my body through the world, and
in my hairline's contour, and when
I speak, it is with a voice that
is within their family of voices.
And so I hold to these remnants,
as if there were all the world's
gold, or love. Barb took a liking
to Bill, took as a challenge I
think, a personal goal, to break
through Bill's remote exterior,
to ferret out that gratitude she

finds in everyone, some unknown
reserve or continent, beneath
the ice, Antarctica's lush past
of tropical memory underneath the
endless depthless cap. It was a
wonder to see, Bill's meltdown
over time. She courted him,
attending to any whim, where one
might be detected, asking his
opinion, asking again and
again, until he must have
thought that he should have one.
Each day Bill got cozier, until—
towards the end of our time there
he was almost a presence in the
house, no longer an absence, or a
refusal. Slowly he gathered
himself on his own behalf,
slowly he recovered interest in
his life, and took to collecting
in the basement the things he
would take to his new home at his
sister's, a box of drill bits,
his snowmobile helmets, his golf
clubs pushed on their cart up
against the table, which everybody
knew that he would never use.
A whole table covered with symbols—
of the past restored to some
small measure of its dignity.
Here were ideas he had had,
or ideas that he might have
had, here were the helmets
that held a man's thought,
when out in a snowbound wilderness

my father and Bill, each on his own
snow machine, pulled from the trail
to assess perhaps the beauty,
and to share a flask. With
the renewal of the interest in his
life, which must have owed itself
to the touch of a woman, which
Bill had never known but for
his mother's, he learned to take
himself seriously, which maybe
he had never done, some innate
integrity which everyone possesses,
dormant for sixty years or more,
in a country that did not take
time, the way Barb did, to
honor it. Parts of us may stay
remote and undeveloped, perhaps
whole people live in only partial
fulfillment, and die unknown and
unmourned, not even themselves knowing
what they were. We had two incredible
nights, after the kids flew home,
alone in the house with Bill.
We made a big production of our
dinners, lots of dishes hot or
warm, the rolls he loved, which
I drove all over town to find,
and wine and candlelight,
and in the dining room, where I
am nearly positive my father
and his brother never ate. It
was all so extravagant— I even let
the old wax candles splatter on
the tablecloth, and Bill had
two good nights, of a returning

appetite. Unhurriedly, for
what was there to hurry for?
when we were all together in
the room, these coconspirators
in how the world was still there
to be met and loved. Bill was
timeless and polite. For an
hour or so each night, of two
in a row, we celebrated what we
were, and celebrated Bill,
catering to his every whim.
I had to keep my eye on Barb
to make sure she did not go
completely overboard, and to
keep my eye on myself for how much
I was overjoyed with finding in
my uncle something to save.
Then he was gone. The people
came for him, and it was quiet
in the house, a terrible quiet,
of nothing to do any longer for
anyone. And then we missed him
and mourned his leaving. He
was one of ours, shaped from
our common clay, and
fashioned with our own hands,
and discovered like some long-
lost fabled land, where even
the people there cannot remember
the glory of their heritage,
of what the sacred objects
scattered all about them mean.
Glazed eyes, hands that do not
move in the old ways, slumped
shoulders, and then one day the

strangers came— as if on chariots—
down from the clouds. So Bill
awakened and took flame.

In the Library

in memory of Delmore Schwartz

Nothing doing. Silence— no— a hum
of the lights. Or is it the air-
conditioning or heat? I am just
completing my work— and look around me
wildly. What?— Is there nothing more?
Of the shape of my day?— poems to read,
classes to get ready for? Without it—
Where would I be? Outside, in the snow,
far from anywhere. Breaking down,
collapsing, as in a Jack London story.
Or, in a different story, in a room,
above a street, in New York City, next
to Delmore, or maybe in that very room.
Bill Zavatsky pointed it out when we
walked. "Up there Delmore died." And
pointed above the boisterous traffic.
When I met that man I thought, somewhere,
I would live like that. Of the mind only—
feeding on words, sucking the life from
words. And if there were no food— you
could write a poem! Or if you were
unhappy— you could write a story
about someone who was more unhappy!
Or maybe very happy. To take what you
were and define it— refine it like
spinning gold out of the dull cold metal
of your life— or music out of fingers
trembling in the dark. I followed Delmore
around one autumn. Kept seeing him on Marshall

Street. Or leaving The Hall of Languages.
He walked briskly in his great coat,
a clutch of books under his arm. Books
like a lunch box. Where later he would open
them and feast. He went in for lunch
one time and I followed him in. We each sat
alone, he over his books, I over mine. In
that instant there in that cheap restaurant
in Syracuse, New York, I became Delmore
Schwartz. To be haunted by him, as I in
turn will do my share of haunting. We
have our matching hideaways, hangouts and
hang-ups. This is one of mine, the Doane Library,
study carrel 1652, or some such number, where
under the hot lights of interrogation,
I make my confession. "The trouble with
Delmore," I can almost hear myself beginning
to say— as if I knew anything until at the
moment it befalls me. To be him, just as
perhaps he was someone else, Baudelaire,
or Joyce, or Kafka. In class he was marvelous.
I have never told this. No one ever asked.
Does no one care to ask?— the way Delmore's
body went unclaimed for days at Bellevue.
He would sit at the front, behind a wall of
books, and talk, not meeting any eyes, but
letting his eyes focus distantly, or perhaps
inside, on the text he was remembering the
joy of— he would talk nonstop— for the
whole hour— no— longer— while I wrote
everything down, not knowing what it was
I wrote. He was a man in love with words,
a bear of a man— look at the size of him,
well fed on air. He was a great gossip,
knew who had had what affair with whom—

and told of his own disasters— the days at
Partisan Review, or teaching at Vassar.
Nobody ever spoke, nobody interrupted. After-
wards, finishing, he rose— and then was gone.
In the time it took me to unkink my arm, and
call back life to my legs, Delmore was out
the door. I might catch a glimpse of him
fleeing down the walkway. Even then no one
spoke, each of us alone with his thoughts.
He breathed passion. The rest was nothing.
His body hung limp around him when he spoke.
We did not look at it. My own body melted
away. I was just ears and my long right
arm, scribbling, and afterwards sometimes
could not make out my scrawl. Each day I
took my visit to the oracle. In his
presence I was comforted. After he left,
the classroom was a cold nowhere. The chair
empty where the magician had sat. Once I
thought of sitting down, ahead of class, to
see how it felt— see if my tongue learned
poetry there. But it was just a chair. Or
I was still myself. Outside, our afternoons
were growing more and more serious about the
grayness of their skies, the hard indifferent
skeletons of trees. We would have to endure it.
Our songbird had flown— down Marshall Street—
dragging his books. No spring again until next
week, when all at once he would flap down in his
great flapping coat to sing once more. So are
born the poets of our time. From under the wings
of such ungainly birds we nurture, far from
our homes, on the edge of this unhappy wilderness
we call the world. Every day was gray in
Syracuse. Slush in the streets, gray cement

walks, gray roads, snow gray in the air. Spring
lived only in the poet's mouth. I never told
him how I loved him. How I took my life from
his. In one semester he gave me everything.
It was all too much. I would take decades to
sort it out. Let me tell you how I have carried
on his tradition. I wear shabby clothes, as he
did. Is it intentional? No, not really, as I
think neither did he wish to offend. We do not
have time, the two of us— to dress ourselves
except in what we have just taken off.
Does the robin alter its daily dress?
He had his Marshall Street, his bar called
The Orange. I have my Sportsman Bar, where
I never drink— just coffee, and come in
desperate in the gray mornings, and am saved.
The smallest gesture links us to the universe.
Cheryl comes by, pours my coffee, and this is
Delmore catching the look in my eye, or hears
the frantic scribbling of my pen. He was
always alone. Or not alone at all. Under his arm
he bore the mind of Joyce, the poetry of Rilke.
Kafka's haunted stories. When he read from
their work there was no need for anything.
It is late now, in the Doane College Library.
Maybe they have the old boy's poems— I should
look some time. He did not become my Joyce,
whose words were blood or breath. Some flaw
in my design keeps the spell from taking full
effect. My solitude I take from my father.
Delmore's poems— when did he have time to
write?— reduce, alas, to a handful. When Tim
Skeen chose his list of readings for his Ph.D. exam
Tim included Delmore. I read the little bit the
Norton has, and then we met to talk, but no

one mentioned him. I can go years doing other
things. But then it hits me all at once— in
the midst of a gray season, a dark November—
whose child it is I am, and then I hear the
poets singing in the spring.

Drinking Beer with Bill Trela

The last to see my brother alive. The
last to breathe in that air he breathed
out. The last who with him could be
wholly distracted, not caring if they
were going anywhere, or what their
lives meant. No interrogations. No
third degree. No scrutiny across the table
at Jeff's hair, disheveled, askew, matted,
flyaway, uncombed, unkempt, who cared!
Beard coming in, unshaved, spattered,
speckled, matted, bristly, ugly, of
course, not caring. Love forgives. The
depth of a friendship. Not being a mother
so as not to poke and pick, meaning pressure,
meaning change!— Do something with yourself
for God's sakes! Neither exasperated nor
mean— not like that, gentle, accepting,
approving, a friend and a friend's hand,
a friend's arms around each other, hugging
in silence, just driving along wrapped in
the silence. The last to sit at a bar—
I see them not at a table but at the bar,
looking at each other reflected in a
mirror, that sort of obliqueness,
sharing a beer at the Stumble Inn,
my father there, on accident, on his
way north, with his brother. Father,
uncle, brother Jeff, and Bill Trela,
four men held in time's embrace.
Where was the world? They could not
be called back. A Friday night, with

Dad just out of work, heading north,
into the cold, into the chill of night
air which lies in shadows of dark
trees, into woodsmoke, mountain
trails, the scent of hemlock which
when you smell it once you want
with you always, and imagine
underarm deodorant squeezed from
the cones, or aftershave, clear as
lake water, to splash on unshaved
cheeks— the odor of forests, the
odor of mothball sweaters Dad and
Bill preserved against the mice, their
whole house smelling of mothballs,
wearing, once, in some bygone era,
wool sweaters Nani had knitted, bright
with snowflake patterns. Snowflakes
and hemlock cones, the bristle of
branch stems, brushing past as you
walk in the woods, the springy
feeling of the needles on the ground,
as if you walked in a padded
universe, where the child no longer
can fall down and skin his knee,
Jeff safe at last beyond recriminations,
beyond the asking who you are, what it
means to be you, what it means
to be twenty-five and out of
work, and have no prospects,
nothing but some drawings in
the basement, of a few knife blades,
a pair of leather saddlebags,
cut out, designed, but still the
stitching left to do, which Father
will finish later for Jeff's

friend who looks just like Sammy Davis
and makes my uncle laugh—
"He looks just like Sammy Davis,"
Bill says, as if it were enough
to say that, as if it were enough
to know that about him, that
not taking somebody seriously,
not caring what their life means,
but not asking either, not asking
for explanations, and that
friend of Jeff's, who took off on
his motorcycle and who I have not
ever seen again— after the funeral,
come back to earth again, come
back to consciousness and my
accounting, my restless mind
trying to add everything up, to
keep account of that friend,
and the smell of hemlock— how can
all these things?— and the
smell of leather?— add up to
nothing in Jeff's death? But
see that friend my brother had,
who took us after the funeral over
to his house nearby my father's,
and put a record on of ecstatic
music, glittering guitars and
violins, and I saw symphonies on
wheels, the whole orchestra astride
their motorcycles, heading off
into the searing sun— that
friend come back reborn alive
in my son's friend, Dukiro Guy,
to whom my son retains his loyalty
through thick and thin, and all

the ways we're led along in
counter movements to the ways our
hearts go, friendship against the
odds, preserving that love my brother
loved, preserved in my son's love.
What is a life but love?
What loves us and what we love,
and, after death, after
a loved one dies, preserved by
love, what love remembers. What
does love remember? The years
drift, the years slide away, the
years are dust in the mouths of
the dead. And you could put my
brother back together, get him all
added up out of all whatever
everybody knows, out of the stories
told of unnamed friends, and people
he bumped into on the way, and
names I know, the sacred ones
of Bidwell, Hinman, Donohue,
Zeman, and he who was last with
him in his earthly form, Bill
Trela, who sat at the bar and
heard Jeff talk, and drank a beer
with him, and got in the car,
and handed Jeff the keys for the
drive back. And "handed Jeff the
keys!— for the drive back!" The law
that everybody knew, you did not let
Jeff drive, this told to me as if in
secret, as if his ways with cars,
notorious, could not be uttered in
a room aloud, but must be whispered.
And not remember who it was

who told me, but at the edge
of some space, some shadowed
realm, where whispers are like
shadows on the soul, where all these
years Bill Trela has lived for me,
not coming out into the light, but
consigned for thirteen years to some
underworld of the unfulfilled,
where error flourishes and dies,
where no one goes to knock upon
the door, a place of darkened corners,
spiders and dust, spiders of spite,
where what is fearful is afraid
and hides. Whose name will not be
uttered in my mother's house, whose
name is never spoken by my father,
for whom it is all now "gone with
the wind." And so I came to ask
at that door, is he within?— whose
name is now synonymous with death.
What does love remember? I ask.
Love that outlasts spite or grief,
love that outlasts anger. Finding,
touching the spot where anger's
bruise was blue, and blackened, and
then, amazed, finding no pain in
the place, knowing I was healed,
at last, alive in my health,
abundantly alive, and having
forgiven the world, I sought Bill
Trela in the place he was keeping
himself, in his mother's house, in
my brother's town, to see how the
world sat with him. Saying—
this is not my brother's murderer.

This is not some stranger on the way
to whom we give some casual regard.
This is where my brother's love went
out as in a mirror at a bar,
and came back to him, arms around
the shoulders, arm in arm, to
sit there side by side in the death
car, and to move beyond, going with
Jeff a little ways into death, as far
as we can, holding our breath the
whole time, holding onto life and
the need to be getting back. I
have sat in that car myself, and
handed Jeff the keys, and let him
drive. And driven on with him,
at breakneck speed, into the
ruin he brought to himself, and
driven on as if by our impact, into
the dark myself. And felt around
in that dark for years, looking
for something I could not give a
name to. Love turns over the
keys to those whose hands reach
out. And I have turned over the
keys to my cars to daughter and
son, and let them drive off into the
night, not knowing if I will see
them again. Trusting that love
will keep them safe till morning.
So I came to have a few beers
with Bill Trela. And picked him
up in my car, and showed him
the seat belts to keep us safe,
alive together in the world
in summer. He was dressed in

a bright white shirt, billowy and
silky, and open down the front,
exposing his chest, as if we were
to be lovers, and going on a date,
looking scrubbed and clean. As if
we would be lovers, going out,
into the dark, and come back
home again, and read me a poem—
a loving poem for Jeff, which
burned in my mind as he read,
the words going in, searing my
mind, the selfsame words that
I had wrestled with— "arms spread/
laughing," of a poem of sharing.
Two poets were we, celebrating a
brother. It was a beautiful night.
We sat out under the stars, under an
umbrella at an open air cafe,
as if to remember Jeff, who always
preferred the open air to anybody's
room, stale and closed in like his
own, which he was always fleeing
from. Bill and I talked about poetry,
about his magazine, and I got
very interested, and would have let
that subject run away with us,
and take my whole energy, until
Bill brought us back at last to talk
of Jeff. I let him talk. And remembered
the time with my brother in my father's
kitchen, with Jeff coming up from
the cellar with beer, and talked
there half the night, the night Jeff
told me all about my poetry.
I told Bill that story, having so

very few to share, but not
bemoaning my fate, accepting what
was, being content with what was.
That was the lesson of this night.
To meet this man without rancor.
To expect nothing, but to be graceful
and kind. To see what love remembered
of the past. To greet this fellow
sufferer and hold him in my arms,
and to survey his wounds. To
see what shame and guilt had wrought,
to touch the scars of grief. We
forgave each other. Two brothers to
Jeff, who through our single and
collective efforts, could not keep him
alive, to sit together under the stars
and be forgiven. Bill was ready
for the evening's necessary turn
of conversation to the burning
question, and gave me some blessed
things to feed my mind in the
off-season, when we would not
be with each other, holding each
other up. Rehearsed, or not,
to tell of my brother being a
poet too, but knowing he was of
a different kind, which he could
live with, all things in the telling
bear special poignancy in a life
that will not be fulfilled,
and we can see our own selves
there, our vanities,
in the mirror held up by the dead.
So we adjust ourselves in that
mirror Jeff holds, weighing our

words, trying to do no harm.
We gave each other gifts of
our attention, who mean so
much to each other we cannot
begin to know all that we mean.
And so we had our night
beneath the stars. Bill would
stagger off to pee every beer
or two, then I'd go, meeting
him on the way back. The
waitress quit at ten, and left
us on our own. Later we went
over to his house and I met
his mother. Bill got out his
attaché case to look for some
manuscripts for his magazine. He
showed me some things, which
turned out to be his own poems.
Then read to me in his beautiful
voice the poem he wrote for Jeff
called "North of Us." Then we
embraced. And then I left. He
walked me out, beneath the stars.
How many times they must have
done this, Jeff and Bill?
How many times they must have
done this, walking out beneath
the stars, not knowing what the
future was. We live in the present.
We do not know what will happen to us.
And so we said goodbye, these two,
these two here, in the middle of the
night, in that place. We would begin
our lives again next morning.
Mother had my breakfast ready,

early, on the table.
Scrambled eggs, and sausage,
toast, juice, coffee and coffee cake.
There were even grapefruits if we
wanted them, each section cut out
for us with a special knife.
It was 7:30 in the morning. We
sat there at the table, Barb and
I and Mom, and rubbed our eyes.
And reached out for the world again.

Getting the Dead Out

Fifteen years of living, the dead pile
up. Is that a dead hand inside
your hand, sweeping around in the sink,
swirling the cloth? Of all the thousand
circuits made and done, dishes eaten
from, plates smashed, the meals we've taken
and digested, keeping the light in our eyes.
The dead pile up. You live in a place,
you move as you did, you sit in the ghost of
who you were, and I stood outside the
other night to piss, and stood there
where another self had stood, what?
ten years ago, rattling around in the shell
of the air which once, shouldered aside,
made room for a brash more impossible self.
We grow accustomed to our place. We
move where we moved, speak where
we might have spoken, shoulder the air
aside, or I sat up one night, late,
reading a book, where fifteen years ago
I stayed up late at night, writing a book.
Getting the dead out. Going out in the yard
and starting the truck. Turning the motor
over of the truck as old as I am, that was 6
when I was twelve, and drove through
all the hurricanes of the spirit, and
kept coming on, Civil Rights, Vietnam,
the murder of John Kennedy, and kept
coming on. It needs a coat of paint,
and I could use some hair. And starts,
to haul off branches from our work.

Fifteen years the bushes have been growing.
New stems leading upwards, climbing towards
the light, new leaves ascending. We
climb toward the light. The branches climb,
and all the while the understory of the house
goes dark. What stands above
shades out the lower limbs.
The father shadows the son, until,
in mad bursting rage or declaration
he breaks forth, to stand in the light.
Each day new dead accumulate. New
cells are old, surrounded or detached.
We make our way on dead paths kept
alive with our going. Today my wife
has plans. She wants to clear out
dead from bushes in our yard. I start
the truck, where earlier I took the
saw and clippers down, and paints
herself with Skin So Soft, over skin
so soft, which chiggers will nest in.
Douses with Cutters Stick, and
pennyroyal oil, to keep the bugs at
bay. Going out for her is
as if for the evening, dressing up
for opera, layering the makeup on.
We go to get the dead out, half dead
ourselves. Halfway to 90, and oblivion,
half our branches underneath
climbing in shadows and to no avail,
we move to make new claims to
an old world. I reach down to
cut away the structure of some
bush, only to see the new green
branches fall and fail, collapse
for all the dead gone now which

used to hold them up. We are
held up by the dead. They shape
our postures in the sun. My
brother, who would be 38 today,
arranges my idea of time.
It is a dozen years now since
his death, and my gray sticks
of beard and hair announce their
deaths. Held by the dead, compelled
in their orbit, compelled to stand
and move in the places of a former
dream. So now I bend in the
old way, yank and pull the
dead out sideways. The dead
are never through with being
dead. They like the evenness,
the ring of it, the knock of
knucklebone on hard dry wood.
Getting the dead out. Cutting
the bushes back. Making room
for the new. It is a complicated
procedure. Barb goes in with
clippers and snips what will yield
to its jaws. Sometimes what she
cuts is green and yields quite easily.
The dead are difficult. You may
get a good start, but soon the
hard dry wood resists the blades, the
cutters jam. That's when I go in
with the saw. The back and forth slow
movement of the teeth, reducing every
pass a little bit, scattering dust,
is how the dead are subdued. Then
the whole long piece must be yanked
out, the bottom cut free, but the

top, where the living of leaf got done,
is all asnarl with other stems.
Living entraps us. We cannot pull
free. Once having done our lives
long enough in a place, among other
lives, we are held in place as if we
were a branch ensnarled with other
branches. We may think ourselves
free, to stand alone in the sun, or
shadow, but when we go to fall, or
quit, we cannot quit, they will not
let us quit, but hold us up by their
own strong habit of living. So Barb
and I lean on each other. So when
we pull one way a little bit the
other feels it and resists. So
we are drawn to each other and
must be together, like someone and
her shadow, like a branch which lies
along another branch, to cast our
shadow down, marking our path, or
as the sun moves, being darkened by
the shadow of the other. At the
top, at the ends, where one conceives
the fingers to be, here are our leaves
ensnarled in the palms of each other,
growing as if as one. Cutting is easy.
The saw moves, the teeth so sharp,
without constraint, fashioned to the
work, relentlessly moves. The trick
is disengaging the dead from the
dead, of disengaging the dead from
the living. So I must be free of
my brother, the shadow which holds
me down, I battle, relentless,

cutting each year free of a little
more. Then somehow the branch
comes free, a huge unshapely reach
of length beyond our wildest dreams.
The dead are extensive. The trials
that living puts to us extend us
in all wild reaches to escape.
And so we go off twisting
in odd ways, reaching to put out
leaves, taking a hold, laying
straight along another branch,
then coming to a corner, trapped,
branching out and taking off again.
There's no way to account for it.
Life is too slow to see. Its
hold, enduring, its tenacity.
Such branches are a nightmare
in the truck, and will not fit the
box. You carry a big armload,
an armload of arms, which has
no weight at all, but is mostly
air, and jam them in the box.
And later must climb up to walk
them down. Once in the air
they were graceful, and whose
leaves sighed in the summer
breeze, which now a nuisance
must be packed and wedged.
The dead must be persuaded,
by force if needed. They do
not surrender. Long after their
joy is done, and what was life
passes into habit and the sun
no longer warms them or brings
on the leaves, the dead remain,

quite visible. They make an
imprint of what was, to shadow
all our days, or give us an idea
for how to dream. What they did
we might do, or we are
doomed to do. The past comes
back again. Irrelevance is here,
just as in life, and here a
branch took off at right angles
to itself, and seemed insane,
but which bore flowers once.
The dead were beautiful. Even
the dry-stick silver of
their bark is lovely, and
the hardness of the wood
scratches my skin and brings
the blood. The dead may wound
us still, far from their power
to please us, or burn brightly
in a fire, soothing the day,
putting an edge to our ambitions.
So Barb and I get the
dead out. She is the brains
behind the project, the
motivator. I am full of
old regrets and sorrows, and
see everything for the emblem
it is. The world asserts its
weight of time and loss, even
in some little air. We cut
some branches in our yard,
while I cut free, or try,
or try to disengage myself,
old, and remembered, and lay
my wrist along the forearm of

a limb, and cut. This is known
as getting the dead out. It
doesn't last. It must be done
again and again. The world
lives and dies. It holds
us in its fast embrace, snagging
our clothes, stabbing out to poke
our eyes. And once I went to
throw a huge nest of limbs
out of the truck and down the
bank into the pit at the dump,
it grabbed my hand and tugged
at me. The dead want company.
They want to pull us down with
them, into the common pit,
drawn to the earth again
after our wild ascents.

The Vision

When I was dying and choking on grief
a vision came to me
a man came to me out of the mist
and I looked and I stared
and I thought
Who is this come to speak to me
and it was my brother in
his black motorcycle jacket
and he said
let not this pain I have given
be wasted on you
if I die then I die so that you
will live better
in the full light of the knowledge
of death
the bird will no longer be the bird
but something which dies
which sings and then stops singing
and the dog you will love
for being faithful and for dying too
for how can we love what does not die
but you will love that too
the rain in the window
the sun that comes over the hill
in the morning
these will be precious to you
clumsily you will move among them
awkward with your newfound knowledge
strangely will you seek out things
and you will want to fill your house
with strange objects

pieces of bark, tree branches, stones,
water that had flown through the air as rain
surrounding yourself with pieces of
the living world
and there will be many who will wonder at you
and pull away
or think you mad
but you should go among them without apology
and make no pretense that
whatever they believe you believe
but that you believe some new thing
that everything there is has mortal taint
and therein beauty lies
but even with mortality we may be wrong
and even with this vision armed though we be
we may go foolishly adrift
and think of petty things
and become angry and selfish
forgetting our task
it is not easy he said
being dead or being with the dead
or being as you are living still
with so much that you love already dead
and if you do not wish to go
into the world again as I instruct you
I will understand

And what will happen to me if I turn
away and ignore you?

Probably nothing will happen.
You will go on struggling
in anger and grief,
and your grief will fly out and become
transformed into anger at others

who do not feel the loss you feel
and your mind will be sharpened against complaints
and your tongue will become pointed and fiery
and you will not forgive the world
and you will make the world pay for your pain
as if it were the world's fault
and perhaps you will become bitter and old
clutching your few things to you
harboring your pain.
Oh you may keep faith with those closest
to you
you may shelter your children in some special
category but you will let them go
and not all knowledge will be foreign to you
because whatever lives must live a graceful life
that even the wounded dog learns how to drag
itself over the ground
and forgets after all to cry out
and you will be happy enough
in your way
saying that what has come to you is how it was
meant to be
that life had dealt the cards and you must play them
even where the cards are not good
and you will make up ways of seeing and saying
to shape your vision of the world
and you will die and be mourned by a handful.

And what will happen to me if I accept
your vision and forgive the world?

Then the world will open for you.
What was closed will open.
The faces of people formerly closed
will open and reveal their cares and their joys.

You will become one who knows from the heart
and walks therefore on stones of light
over the flowing ribbons of the world.
People will speak and you will hear affection
in their voices and you will hear how their
fears stand there naked in their mouths
and you will reach out to them
because they are mortal things
and put them at ease.
A restlessness will fill you.
Life will be good but there will never be
enough of it.
Good or bad whatever happens
you will be ready, you will be responsive.
This one death will enable you to
live at the fullest reach of your self.
Loving all men and women and children
of the world.
The beggar will be no less to you than the
beautiful child,
man or woman, rich or poor,
you will accept them in their freshest selves,
even the one who has gone crazy
you will find comfort in and meaning
and the one who has killed in anger or fear
you will find ways to forgive.
The old will have a special place in your heart
and the very young, but most you will
reserve your pleasure for those like yourself
seeing how blended all the many forces are
in them, the children they are, the old people
they are growing into,
and even more if that is possible
there will be special joy in those
from whom you have become estranged,

your father for instance,
or someone once you hated or who did you wrong
across that gulf and barrier of hate
you will build bridges to walk on
avenues of understanding and forgiveness.

And so will I come to forgive even
you, my brother who died?

That shall be your greatest achievement.
Others will seem as nothing compared to this.
Where once I was a dark wall around you and over you
I will become a doorway of light.
Where once I was all you could not resolve of
the past or put to rest
I will become the edge of the future unfolding
and questing, the lip that breaks the sea,
that leads us forward into the new world.
So long have you looked back and poked
amidst the dirt and weeds
it will be hard to straighten up and walk.
And you will have come to enjoy your bent form
and your shuffling gait
and you may resent being stirred from your long sleep
but when you have lifted yourself and are gone
the way will become precious to you and
you will never ever want to stop
and when at last you too must die
you will lie down glad for the world
forgiving and forgiven.

And then the air was still.
The other speaker vanished, the vision was over.
That was a long time ago.
Or it never happened.

Kuzma

I went on with my dying, as all men do,
went on with my grieving, as I intended.
Went on doing what I knew to do, or failing
tried another thing which also failed,
until at last having tried them all
I was free of these illusions and alternatives,
and came at last to the end of my wits
the end of my struggle and surrendered.
And fell asleep exhausted from my long denials.
And woke like Scrooge on Christmas Day,
amazed there was still life to live,
a day to be saved from the darkness,
and so my life began again.

About The Poet

Greg Kuzma has been teaching poetry writing classes to undergraduates at the University of Nebraska since the autumn of 1969. After a slow start of about 20 years, these past 20 years he has begun to figure out how it needs to be done.

The poems in *All That is Not Given is Lost* were written from 1988 through 1995.

In 1995 Greg began trying to teach himself how to write screenplays. He has completed 15, none of which has been produced.

In 2003 his colleagues in the Department of English encouraged him to try his hand at writing shorter poems again. Some of these new poems will appear shortly in *Iowa Review, Paterson Literary Review,* and *Plains Song Review.*

Greg has been the faculty advisor to the undergraduate literary and fine arts magazine, *Laurus,* since 1995. During these years *Laurus* went from an annual issue of 80 pages to issues over 200 pages and one at 300 pages and one at 400 pages. *Laurus* is edited entirely by undergraduates, and publishes only undergraduates at UNL. Currently at press is issue 06/07. Issue number 07/08 will be printed over the summer and will be available for use in fall classes. *Laurus* publishes stories, poems, plays, parts of novels, book reports, film criticism, literary scholarship,and personal essays as well as drawings, photographs and prints— "anything so long as it's good." Each issue comes with a full-color cover.

Greg's tenure as advisor will end with issue 07/08.

Greg is married to Barbara and they are the parents of a son, Mark, and a daughter, Jacquelyn. Mark is a freelance computer programmer working out of San Diego, California. Jacquelyn is the office manager at Trane Heating and Air Conditioning in Ft. Collins, Colorado, and is the mother of Alexis Sky Kuzma Bartlett.. Barbara is the enrichment teacher of the Crete Public Schools, and is presently working at all levels. At the levels of senior high and middle school she is assisted by college professors from Doane College in Crete.

The cover title for this book was hand-written by The Amazing Baby Alex. The background "ABCs" is the famous work-page Alex created three or four years ago, and is one of Greg and Barb's favorite works of art.

Greg and Barb reside in Crete, Nebraska, with their orange cat, Emerson.

CPSIA information can be obtained at www.ICGtesting.com
Printed in the USA
LVOW13s0835121113

360980LV00001B/123/A

9 780978 578275